The No BS Divorce

—

Secrets of a Divorce Attorney

by Brigid A. Duffield, Esq.

The No BS Divorce, Secrets of a Divorce Attorney
by Brigid A. Duffield, Esq.

ISBN 978-0-98-19669-0-8
Library of Congress Cataloging-in-Publication Data
First Edition

Duffield, Brigid A.
The No BS Divorce, Secrets of a Divorce Attorney / Brigid A. Duffield
Printed in the United States of America

Published by Legally Speaking, Inc.
1749 S. Naperville Road
Wheaton, IL 60189

Copyright 2009

Cover by Kristin Richey, www.kristinrichey.com

Graphics by Marilyn Dale, www.marilyndale.com

Legally Speaking, Inc. books are available at special quantity discounts to use as premiums or for educational training programs. For more information, please contact Legally Speaking, Inc. at 630-221-9300.

To arrange for a media interview or speaking engagement, call 630-221-9300.

www.brigidduffield.com

"This is the best single-source book on how to get a divorce without going crazy! It should be read by anyone contemplating or going through a divorce."

Brigid opened my eyes to what getting a divorce really involves and what I am actually paying for.

She offers the information you need, without the BS! to make going through a divorce a little bit easier."

When Brigid speaks, people listen. This book is a definitive collection of tips, information, and stories designed to get you thinking and keep you sane during a divorce or family transition.

"I consulted with several attorneys and after reading this book I knew what questions to ask and what I needed to do to help my attorney get it done.

"This book is amazing! I read it and now I'm reading it again. Thank you for making such a difficult process easy to read and understand."

"This book caused me to re-evaluate how I approached many aspects of my divorce and my life. This message is clear and compelling. I think this book is going to make a big difference. I wish I read it before I got divorced"

Important Disclaimer: Before you read this book, please be aware that nothing in this book suggests that someone should get a divorce without consulting with or retaining an attorney. Attorneys are the vital link in the process that ensures that the agreements reached are actually reflected in the legal documents. Although this book is made to ensure a "No BS divorce," this publication is sold and read with the understanding that the author, editors and publishers are not responsible for the result of any action taken on the basis of information in this work, nor for any errors or omissions. The publishers and the authors and editor, expressly disclaim all and any liability to any person, whether a purchaser of this publication or not, in respect of anything and of the consequences of anything done or omitted to be done by any such person in reliance, whether whole or partial, upon the whole or any part of the contents of this publication, If expert advice is required, services of competent professional persons should be sought.

About the Author

An expert in divorce and mediation, Brigid A. Duffield has written articles which have been publish in the *American Bar Association Judge's Journal, American Journal of Family Law, The Illinois State Bar Journal and the DuPage County Bar Brief.*

Since 1984 Brigid has been in private practice concentrating in family law and domestic relations, financial disputes, custody disputes, child representative and guardianship appointments including related matters. Brigid has represented more than 1,100 clients involving complex legal issues relate to dissolution of marriage, real estate, custody support issues, taxes, pensions, business valuations.

She also has specialized experience and skills in mediation, having mediated more than 1,000 family law matters. Highly skilled in conflict resolution, she played a major role in the development of what is now the Illinois State Model and 18th Judicial Circuit mandatory mediation program for family law and the DuPage County Bar Association mediation referral program.

Brigid provides information to better understand the quirks of the legal system. She dispels the myth that the legal system will deliver what appears to be the logical result. She will help you identify and develop certain skills that are critical from the client's perspective. In addition, she shares ways to enhance critical relationships inside and outside the legal system.

Acknowledgments & Special Thanks to the Technical Reviewers

The *No BS Divorce, Secrets of a Divorce Attorney* was reviewed and edited by my dear friends and colleagues Bob Adams, Kathleen Fee, Sandy Kaczmarski, Lesle Koepp, Bill McCartney, Chris Regan and Pam Terry. These guiding lights are people who I would not normally mix with, yet alone love and without whom my ability to write this book would have been impossible. They not only checked the accuracy and readability of what you'll learn in this book but also provided insight and guidance to help ensure that this book gives you a practical, easy to read guide with everything you need to know to have a "No BS Divorce."

The book you are reading is the result of knowledge, advice and feedback shared by a group of extremely talented people. Throughout this book you will read advice I have learned from clients, therapists, Judges, attorneys and mediators. Excellent advice has also come from those well intended relatives who really want what's best for the family, even if the advice doesn't match the facts. In this book you will learn from the numerous experiences I have encountered in my twenty five years practicing family law. The step-by-step advice is here to help you achieve you own success while going through a divorce. Success being keeping the money in your family, keeping you out of court once the matter is closed, limiting the possibility that your children will become our next litigants.

My assistants, Jessica Geib, Kylie Hannon, Rachel Cegielski, Megan Eshelman and Kelly Kuhlman, edited this book and organized it so the information would be most useful for the reader. Their help was invaluable. Special thanks to my colleagues at the National Speaker's Association, Maureen O'Brien, Conor Cunneen, Johnny Campbell, Sherrin Ross Ingram, John Walsh, Lillian Bjorseth, Steve Beck, Deanne DeMarco, Steve Steinberg and Cheryl Kuba, who held me accountable for completing this book.

For my Husband Ken, my daughter Patricia, our German Shepard Callie, my parents Joe & Ann and my siblings, Peggy (& Sam), Sheila (& Paul), Mary, Pat (& Katy), Ann (& Tony) Terry and Eileen (& Tim) for without their love and support this journey would not have been possible.

The No BS Divorce—Secrets of a Divorce Attorney

To:

_____

From:

_____

The No BS Divorce—Secrets of a Divorce Attorney

Contents

The No BS Divorce—Secrets of a Divorce Attorney

The No BS Divorce
Secrets of a Divorce Attorney

100 or More Secrets and Tips to Keep Your Money in Your Family While Getting a Divorce

Forward

"Life is difficult"

"This is a great truth, one of the greatest truths. It is a great truth because once we truly see this truth, we transcend it. Once we truly know that life is difficult—once we truly understand and accept it—then life is no longer difficult. Because once it is accepted, the fact that life is difficult no longer matters."

—M. Scott Peck from
"The Road Less Traveled"

Divorce is difficult. When M. Scott Peck wrote *The Road Less Traveled,* he could have easily been talking about going through a divorce. Perhaps then the opening sentence would have been: *Divorce is incredibly difficult.* This is a great truth. Once we really understand it, we can accept it and we can do something about it.

1

Divorce is difficult:
- For the individual
- For the spouse
- For the children
- For the extended family
- For the friends
- For the employer
- For the co-workers
- For the lawyer
- For the dog, for the pets
- For everyone touched by the person contemplating divorce.

Why Marriages Fail

In the "olden" days, people vowed they would stay to-gether "until death do us part." Why is the commitment different when couples make those same vows today? I don't know. I suspect the reason is that in those days of old, people didn't live as long as we live today. One partner would die before reaching thirty. They did not live to see children, grand-children or great grandchildren. Many mothers died in child birth. Many fathers were killed in battle. But this book is not about the why or the how commitments fail…that is better left to those who like to analyze extensively. I have found it doesn't matter.

My expertise and talents involve getting people in and out of the legal system as quickly as the family can tolerate. My strengths include identifying areas of current and future conflict; helping couples figure out which conflict resolution skills can work best for the individuals involved; how to apply those skills to problem solving and negotiations and identifying how and which of these skills will help them overcome long-standing difficulties in the future. I hope to empower people to gain the skills they need to be able to continue to deal with the person they were formerly married to. Having those skills makes it easier to attend parent-teacher conferences together, share their kids' big days (birthdays, graduations and weddings) and have a better working relationship with their next partner or spouse.

We live in a time when, statistically, a marriage is more likely to fail than to succeed. Not all marriages fail for the same reason and the breakdown of a marriage doesn't usually happen because of only one reason. Nevertheless, there are some reasons which seem to occur more frequently and are more evident than others. Poor communication, financial problems, lack of commitment, a dramatic change in priorities, changes in personalities, lives added, lives taken away, infidelity, addiction and substance abuse fall within the most common reasons. We lawyers see other causes although perhaps not quite as frequently as those listed above. Those other causes include failed expectations or unmet needs, physical, sexual or emotional abuse and almost always a lack of conflict resolution skills and no desire to learn them.

The National Center for Health Statistics reports that 43 percent of first marriages end in separation or divorce within fifteen years. In my office, I frequently consult with spouses who have been married for fifteen years. Those people often take another two years of thinking about their commitment to the marriage before ultimately wanting to end the marriage by the time their seventeenth wedding anniversary arrives. Many marriages end at seventeen years. When one partner makes the decision to separate it is usually made after a long period of time and careful consideration of the outcomes.

The emotional torment of thinking about and weighing the pros and cons of the decision often takes years, although for some it seems like it just happened. Individuals who are considering a divorce often contemplate, question and rethink the decision privately. They don't talk about it with friends or family. At some point, they may begin to state the idea of a divorce publicly. They begin to talk about it at work and with trusted friends. They make it a little public. Then, depending upon the feedback from these advisors, they either see value in reconciliation or they see hope in a separation.

In my experience, no one wakes up one day and says "Life is good. I have a great spouse, a great family—I think I will move out or get a divorce." The decision to divorce creates challenges, anger, fear, resentment and hatred not only for the person making the decision, but for the members of the family affected and the people the family touches. But the trauma and long-term detrimental effects of divorce can be reduced dramatically when both the person considering a divorce and the person upon whom the divorce is being imposed are able to step back, see what needs to be done and proceed in a manner which considers both their positions.

Then when they are in the legal process of the divorce, they will get through the legal process with less time, less pain, less expense and more ability to move on with their lives. When people understand that in the legal setting, the divorce courtroom, it doesn't really matter why someone wants a divorce, it is easier. It is hard to believe that there is no right, wrong, good or bad reason for the divorce.

It does not seem logical that someone shouldn't have to pay for the decision, either financially or otherwise. But the truth is people are not penalized because they want a divorce. They don't have to offer a logical explanation. It just happens. And, absent divine intervention, it is my experience that reconciliation is no longer possible and there is no going back once a person has made that final decision.

Many of us teach our children basic principles of living, values and the golden rules. We tell our children "do unto to others," "work it out" and "talk to the other person" when they are in conflict with a friend. But when it comes to conflicts leading to a divorce, it is almost impossible for someone who wants a divorce to live by those rules. It is too hard to be nice, it is too difficult to talk to the other person and it is difficult to work things out. Then when the spouse who is being divorced sees the problem, any attempt to save the marriage is met with the reality that their efforts to restore the marriage are "too little too late."

One of the facts most misunderstood by people getting a divorce is that if they have children, they are never really separated. Yes, they are divorced as Husband and Wife. But, the reality is that most divorcing couples will be forever joined and bonded together as Mom and Dad. It is important to recognize that those relationships will continue and they will continue to be rocky. Until the parties understand that getting a divorce is not the end of a relationship but, in fact, the beginning of a new relationship with someone they don't like, they will not acquire the skills they need to continue to work with, negotiate with and problem solve with their former spouse. It will be difficult to show up at a son's basketball game or a daughter's ballet recital knowing the other parent is there. It will be impossible to sit together and cheer for the child or the child's team. It will create confusion and perhaps a "split" for the child who may feel that any affection shown for one parent in the presence of the other is a clear betrayal.

For the sake of raising healthy children who will not become my next clients or the court's next litigants, I have a very specific philosophy that positively impacts the manner in which families go through a divorce, manage their family and financial reorganization and acquire the skills needed to continue to have a relationship with their former spouse.

When a marriage suffers a breakdown so severe that divorce is contemplated and perhaps necessary, spouses lose sight of the common goals and common likes and dislikes they once had. The very differences that attracted them in the first place become fatal flaws in the relationship. In a successful marriage, it can sometimes be difficult to get a Husband and Wife on the same page at the same time on a certain issue. In a divorce, a Husband and Wife are almost never on the same page at the same time. Then when the voices of all the other players—children, in-laws, friends and other relatives —begin to chime, chaos is sure to reign.

My hope is that this quick read and easy reference book will help those men and women who want to preserve their integrity, financial resources, emotional well-being, mental health and sanity. I hope the guidelines set out in this book will help them move forward with grace and dignity...at least some of the time, at best most of the time.

These guidelines are for those people who hope that when the pain of a divorce or separation dissipates, they will be able to dance together at their children's weddings and stand together in the hospital nursery to welcome their grandchildren. These guidelines form a plan that will sustain the test of time because they can fluctuate when additional new relationships, new boyfriends, new girlfriends and perhaps new spouses become part of the family. This plan will help parents teach children good conflict resolution skills because they will be watching the two most important people in their lives model effective problem solving. These problem solving skills are as simple as sometimes just agreeing to disagree and ultimately respecting each other's differences.

This book will dispel some of the myths about the divorce process—the "BS," if you will—that creates havoc for the family. This book will dispel some of the myths that cause hurt feelings, excruciating pain, hatred and unnecessary delays in and out of the legal system.

A secret...when the legal delays can be managed and even avoided, the healing that is necessary to effectively co-parent can begin between the spouses. That healing is necessary when parents want to share and attend family events, like team sports events, high school and college graduations, children's weddings and grandchildren's births. Without that healing, unresolved hatred and anger will harm the long-term relationship so that even if it were possible to attend and suffer in silence, the children won't want them there.

I hope to shatter those myths that mystify the legal system. I hope to clear up some common misunderstandings about the legal system. I hope to explain why people will almost always fail in the divorce court room when they think logically. I hope this information will help people, perhaps you, embrace the reality of a wanted or unwanted divorce quickly rather than slowly. This information may even evoke compassion and forgiveness when a divorce is imminent.

The book is organized by individual topic so that each chapter can stand alone or be used as part of a whole. The intention is for you, the reader, to take what you need and leave the rest. Practical tips are provided to give information in a usable fashion, to give guidance, to minimize the trauma and to make divorce a little less difficult.

After practicing family law for more than a quarter of a century, I see firsthand that family separation, seemingly random and without explanation, has immense, long-term damage on all the players named above. I hope to offer long-term solutions to a short-term, temporary problem and to minimize the incredible damage divorce has on relationships, relationships that need to function successfully into the future.

This book will focus on getting through the several, very difficult legal processes that can be made more difficult by emotional, spiritual, physical and mental impairments. It will explain and dispel some of the myths that keep families in various legal processes longer than emotionally or financially prudent. I hope to expose simple secrets that will keep money in your family and facilitate a cost-effective divorce that your family can financially tolerate. Knowing the truth about what needs to be done, when it needs to be done, how it needs to be done, what can't be done and what really doesn't matter will minimize the trauma of divorce on the lives of the person it touches.

Speaking of cost, in addition to actual dollars to be spent, I will discuss the cost of the adversary system, the cost of never knowing the truth and the cost of knowing that your version of reality may never matter to anyone but you. The true cost of the loss of peace of mind and the cost of needing to connect in relationships is by far the greatest.

We will now start the winding journey of making the decision to get a divorce and where that decision will take someone down the road, hopefully less traveled. If divorce is the plan, I hope this book will empower someone you love.... or maybe you....to have an easier walk down its path.

Brigid A. Duffield

P.S. The expression "Bull Sh**" is offensive and crude. I grew up in an environment where swearing was taboo. Of course, as kids we swore for "shock value." As I got older, I discovered it was not necessary to use crude language. The expression "BS" can be offensive to me and to others and for that I apologize. So why did I use that expression? What do I really mean when I say "the No BS Divorce?" I mean that something is ridiculous, idiotic, a half-truth or just stupid. It could refer to any number of negative ideas and actions. The dictionary defines BS as nonsense, especially foolish insolent talk. For me, I think BS is just a "Blarney Statement."

Chapter One:
The Decision...It's Going to Cost You Time, Emotion, Sleep

The decision to divorce is not one I have ever seen any person take lightly or make quickly. At some point in many marriages, even solid, healthy ones, one partner has a passing, fleeting thought that they would like a divorce, that life would be so much better if they were divorced. In that instance, the person snaps out of their fantasy, typically recoiling at the thought. They remember and perhaps make a quick mental list of all the benefits of marriage in general and being married to their spouse specifically. They usually minimize the situation(s) that made them think about the possibility of divorce. They tell themselves and perhaps believe that their marriage is not that bad, that the conflicts are normal, that they are manageable and even that their spouse will change. They consider the consequences of getting a divorce. They fear the potential negative impact on the children. The time it will take, the amount of money it will cost all deter them from really seriously wanting to get a divorce. Then they become the martyr for the cause. They philosophize: "I can do this...'til death do us part."

People come into my law office in various stages of thinking about, considering, contemplating and making the decision to separate or divorce. Often by the time people cross the threshold of any divorce lawyer's office, they have gone back and forth, struggling to make a decision, especially the divorce decision many times. They have replayed the possible impact of a divorce on their lives and the lives of people around them hundreds of times. They have thought about what life would be like without their current spouse. Some have given considerable thought to what they want to do and the potential financial consequences of their action on them as well as on their spouse. They believe they have communicated their displeasure with their spouse or worse, they believe if their spouse cared about them, they would know they were dissatisfied. These people may have often been thinking about the decision and the process for years. There are those too, who come to a divorce attorney's law office because a divorce is being imposed upon them. They never saw a problem in the marriage or they never thought the problems were insurmountable. They thought their spouse was kidding when they complained about something. They didn't take their spouse seriously. They believed "'til death do us part." They never contemplated a separation or a divorce. They feel completely powerless and at a loss for what to do.

Talk about difficult. Usually the first time the thought of divorce creeps into someone's mind, they physically recoil, like a snake in a basket. They frequently seek counseling either from friends or professionals. Over a period of time, however, that nagging, persistent idea keeps creeping up. Everyone who is seriously considering a divorce has wrestled with the notions: "I love him/her. We have kids. We can't afford it. Mom will be upset. I will…[insert your own particular hell here]." Some people question: "Have I done enough? Have I really communicated my unhappiness to my spouse?

Will he/she change? I know I told him/her, but did he/she understand I was serious? Did I send a mixed message? Did he/she hear what I said?" These questions slowly wear away the faithful resolve to stay married. And worse, some think if it's 'til death do us part...I might kill my spouse.

Making the decision to separate or divorce is not a final one. Even after people come to a law office and get the information they need to make the decision to divorce and move forward, they often rethink the decision. Someone who is contemplating separation and divorce makes a series of small decisions over a long period of time.

It can be best described by this simple graphic:

DIVORCE: THOUGHT PROCESS

Thinking about divorce...

We've got kids.

I love my spouse.

What will Mom say?

Other concerns...

After suffering in silence and perhaps even praying about it, they then begin to talk about it with all sorts of safe people, their trusted friends. Most people begin to talk, confidentially at first, to their trusted advisors (close friends, family members). They may go to counseling. Their trusted advisors, very well-intentioned people, begin to give them advice about marriage in general and then about their marriage.

Although well intended, this advice is also presumptuous. The advisors presume some facts, based upon their own values and belief systems. They usually do not have a complete, neutral frame of reference from which to draw. This advice can be further tainted by the potentially inaccurate information provided by the person seeking the guidance. Many times, the information given is skewed in favor of the person seeking the advice and telling the story. So of course the advised is skewed. Most good friends and family members and lots of other people have an opinion, or worse, experience and therefore believe they can give expert advice on what their friend or family member should or should not do when considering a divorce. They want to share those opinions and offer sage advice. Most people give advice in a sincere attempt to spare their friend or loved one from the hell of a divorce like they personally experienced or walked through with one of their friends or family members. But, they frequently misunderstand the facts as they relate to this marriage and they misapply the laws that apply, because they are not divorce lawyers. Advice is sometimes given based upon someone's sense of right and wrong. They may apply logic. The well-intended advice friends and family give may range from "talk to him/her, tell him/her what you are thinking," to "talk to a counselor" to "kick the son-of-a-bitch out the door now." Much of this is BS.

Here's an example: Shannon's best friend Erin got "everything" in her divorce. Shannon thinks she should get "everything" in her own divorce. Erin tells Shannon to fight for everything. So, Shannon embarks on a costly litigation process, only to end up with a garden variety, relatively predictable settlement. This is a fair settlement by legal standards, but a settlement that was certainly not "everything" as she got about half of the assets. Why? What happened? To begin with, Erin's advice was based on her own situation and facts. Her facts did not apply to Shannon's situation. Erin's Husband, feeling guilty for having an affair, was more than happy to give Erin everything, just so he could get out of the marriage and not feel guilty. Shannon's Husband on the other hand, having no reason to feel guilty and not feeling guilty, just wanted to get a divorce and keep his half of everything they acquired during the marriage. Erin certainly meant well, but the facts of her situation were never going to result in the same settlement for Shannon. Shannon paid dearly, financially, time-wise, emotionally and physically to find that out.

No matter where the person is in the process of considering a divorce, all sorts of people have lots of advice and whether or not someone solicits it, the divorce dialog begins. When these dialogs begin, if not sooner, a divorce lawyers should be consulted. This is No BS.

At some point, and it happens frequently after the idea of divorce becomes more than idea but instead a discussion point, the thought of divorce has turned from a Momentary fleeting idea to a persistent, nagging thought. It is at this stage that it is so persistent that the other spouse is completely defenseless against the divorce. Reconciliation, although possible, becomes less and less likely. It is usually no longer an option. The person making the decision has generally reached the point of no return. No matter what their spouse does, it will never be good enough. No amount of counseling or promises to change will work. Moreover, because of the adversarial and intensely personal nature of the issues and disputes between them, the damage is irreparable. It is now when most people cannot make the necessary changes that will be enough to short-circuit or stop the demise of the relationship.

Too often, when people are contemplating a divorce, they mistakenly think their spouse will see the light once the divorce is over or when they are in two homes. They think their spouse will suddenly change all his or her character defects and become the Husband, the Wife, the father or the mother they wanted in the family. That is BS. After the divorce, the same character defects that typify each spouse do not go away…they remain. The defects do not change just because the spouses divorced. During the breakdown of the marriage, lines of communication are closed, relationships are severed, trust vanishes and both spouses ultimately lose credibility, demonstrating less and less integrity during the breakdown of the marriage. Why? Because people are human and because most people don't really change. The same coping and processing techniques that drove a spouse crazy in the marriage will be the same ones that will be present in the separation, divorce and after the divorce.

For people struggling with this monumental decision, the ability to sort out the wheat from the shaft can mean the difference in whether or not reconciliation is possible. If the person has the ability and the emotional freedom to change their mind, save face if you will, they may decide to stay in the marriage and make it work. Sometimes, these seemingly obvious things are the vital links between the possibility of reconciliation and the reality of a very, very nasty separation or divorce.

Often when one spouse reaches the decision to separate, the other spouse is truly caught off-guard, even if the proverbial "writing on the wall" may have been written with graffiti paint. The unsuspecting spouse will always be playing emotional catch-up and sometimes financial and mental catch-up as well. He or she has a much shorter timeframe to process what may have taken the other spouse years to decide.

DIVORCE: THOUGHT PROCESS

This is taking so long...

Thinking about divorce...

We've got kids.

I love my spouse

What will mom say?

Other concerns...

How did this happen?

I love my spouse.

How will I afford it?

Ready for divorce.

This is happening so fast!

The ability to choose whether to stay in the marriage has been removed from this spouse. These spouses are powerless in the decision. There is really nothing they can do to force their partner to reconcile. This powerlessness can manifest as frustration, delay tactics, inappropriate communication with the children or, worse, the use of children as confidants. These manifestations can mean all sorts of other conflict-creating behavior that further deteriorates an already strained relationship. It leads to many sleepless nights. This behavior leads the other spouse to seek legal remedies. It makes it easier for the spouse to proceed with the divorce and it confirms what they knew all along…the marriage was dead.

How can that very expensive, very harmful process be stopped? One way to manage the emotion, the costs and the process is to understand how to navigate and even manage the legal processes and the legal system. Those details are explained further in Chapter Six. That understanding is particularly important for situations where the Mom and Dad relationship will continue, even although the Husband and Wife relationship is ending.

Chapter Two:
The Money...It's Going to Cost You

Money Matters, Tips for Effectively Using Your Billable Time

People are reluctant to really consider the full financial cost of divorce. It is really overwhelming and hard to think about dividing assets, giving some to therapists, some to attorneys and some to financial advisors. People underestimate the cost of setting up and separating into two households. They sometimes wishfully hope that a reluctant spouse will magically pack their bags and move quietly away, happy to lodge in the local YMCA or other interim housing after having borrowed money from their friends and family instead of the marital coffers.

People frequently fail to account for the extra therapy and counseling sessions that their spouse, their children and they themselves may need to work through the emotional trauma. They underestimate the cost of health insurance for the spouse who will no longer be a dependent and who will require his/her own health insurance policy. They confuse a retainer quoted by an attorney for the full cost of the litigation process. They don't hear the attorney when they explain that the retainer is usually only enough to secure their lawyer, start the process, prepare the preliminary paperwork and open the client file. They don't consider the true cost of litigation, a case that goes to trial. They often don't believe or can't imagine that the retainer will be a paltry percentage of the final cost when two attorneys, court costs, a *guardian ad litem* (a lawyer who represents the children's interests), mediation, custody evaluation, financial experts, appraisals and trial have been involved.

Most people have the general idea or may even know that getting a divorce will be expensive. They realize that the attorney-client relationship is a very expensive one. People have heard the exaggerated and distorted stories about attorneys who received large sums of money, large enough to pay for a four-year college education for their child. They have heard tales of the attorney who seemingly did nothing on their client's file.

In truth, the lay person does not understand what their attorneys are doing and what they are actually paying for. To the lay person who is unfamiliar with the legal process, it seems as if they go to court, spend a half-day or more of their life waiting in a hall and then leave the courthouse, still not divorced. Clients sometimes start with a bad impression of lawyers and the false idea that attorneys will take their money and leave them high and dry. This is BS.

All lawyers, and divorce lawyers in particular, work very hard to do a great job for their clients. They are doing it at a time in their client's life when the client is usually at his/her absolute worst. They don't know that most divorce lawyers carry their client's financially and allow clients a lot of time and latitude to pay their bills, even when there is a large outstanding balance on their account.

People often don't understand what their lawyers' actual jobs are, why their lawyers charge them for certain things and what they are paying their lawyer to do. Worse, they don't ask us, their lawyers, questions about it. For example, clients often use attorneys as a sounding board about their day-to-day, non-legal issues, a relatively expensive conversation, instead of having that same common sense discussion with a trusted friend for the cost of a cup of coffee. The difference between a lawyer's advice and a friend's advice is that a lawyer's advice is that lawyer's stock-in-trade. This stock-in-trade is what clients pay for. That is what a client hires a lawyer to do. Using a lawyer as a best friend is a very expensive friendship.

Attorney fees typically range in cost from $200 to $600 dollars per hour. Some attorney fees are higher. Most clients just expect that they will pay an attorney to file for divorce and that it will be enough to end their union. Most clients don't understand the legal process or what really happens when they are in it. In the legal process, the Judge is looking for and wants settlement documents. Those settlement documents are the written agreements relating to the children (a parenting agreement) and the settlement documents relating to the finances (the marital settlement agreement). It is those documents that the Judge is looking for.

When these documents are finalized, the Judge will finalize the divorce. When clients understand that once they are in a courtroom, who did what to whom and why they are getting a divorce is not as important as how are they going to parent their children when they are living in two homes and how are they going to divide up the assets and the liabilities acquired during the marriage. When people can focus their time, energy and financial resources on getting those disputes resolved, documents negotiated and agreed upon, the divorce is usually done.

People frequently underestimate the length of time it takes to get a divorce. They know it can take a long time. In some jurisdictions, the legal process can take as much as 18 months to two years. Statistically, it takes about 18 months from the time a divorce is filed until the time the divorce is finalized...unless the parties take charge of their timeline. When they take charge of the timeline, they can be divorced sooner.

That timeline does not take into consideration the months and years that preceded the legal process, the time when the family was in transition because one partner was contemplating a divorce.

If settlement terms about the assets, liabilities and children's issues are proposed, negotiated, agreed upon, put in writing and signed by both parties, it is possible to be divorced fairly quickly, 30 to 90 days. And that is No BS.

TIMELINES

TRADITIONAL DIVORCE - Often takes 18 months or more

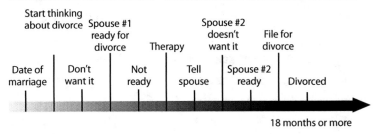

No BS DIVORCE - May take only 30 days

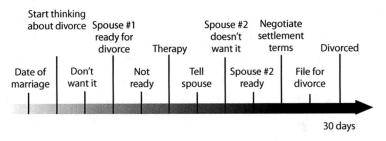

People begin the legal process by retaining a lawyer. A lawyer is retained when a client pays an agreed amount of money for the lawyer to start to work on their matter. Many people have the mistaken belief that a retainer is the full, the entire amount they will have to pay the lawyer. This is BS. A retainer is not an indication of the overall cost of the divorce, it is merely the starting point. A retainer initiates the relationship. It includes hiring and involving a lawyer for the limited number of hours the hourly rate covers.

Once a lawyer has been retained, clients often hope their lawyer can compel their spouse to take action to make their life easier. They often want the lawyer or Judge to force their spouse to take action, even although the client themselves could not compel their spouses to do that. The clients secretly wish and mistakenly believe that lawyers can and will strike so much fear into people that their spouses will just roll over and become sensible. That is BS.

Clients frequently have little understanding of the legal process. The understanding they have is often distorted and inaccurate. Even worse, they don't know that they don't know or understand the process. As a result, clients may not know what questions to ask their lawyers. Clients apply logic and reason to the legal process. For them, it is logical to think that once they file for divorce, they will get in front of a Judge and get it over with and be divorced in relatively short order. That is BS.

In truth, once a case is in the court system, there are only a few ways in which the lawyer can finalize the matter so the client can get divorced in short order...short order being less than 18 months.

Filing prematurely for divorce is the most expensive way to get divorced. It takes the longest amount of time. In my opinion, filing prematurely is when someone files for divorce before the settlement agreements have been finalized. In addition to being expensive, filing prematurely is frequently the least productive and most emotionally destructive process to get a divorce. Filing for divorce starts a series of legal procedures which must be complied with. The procedures are the long way to take to get a settlement. They are in place to get a court case ready for trial and each of the procedures is needed to prepare the Judge, the lawyers and the litigants for a trial Even before any of these steps have to be taken, both parties have to be in the game so to speak. So, the easiest way to get a spouse in the legal system is to serve them by the sheriff. The mere act of being served by the sheriff creates its own set of emotional conflicts that can delay settlement and the divorce by three to four months. Here's an example.

Margaret Mary wanted to get her divorce over and Patrick was unwilling to do anything. She couldn't talk to him about settlement terms and he refused to get a lawyer. Margaret Mary's lawyer suggested that in order to get the case moving, he should have Patrick served by the sheriff. Margaret Mary agreed. The sheriff went to Patrick's job site and served him in front of his co-workers. Patrick was embarrassed, the coworkers' reactions ranged from shock to sympathy. Thereafter, whenever Margaret Mary and Patrick got into a discussion that Patrick didn't want to talk about, he would remind Margaret Mary that she embarrassed him at work by sending the sheriff and he could no longer talk to her about it. This doesn't seem like it should be a problem, but it is. It is a problem that will continue years after the divorce is over. Most people never forget where and when they were served by the sheriff or how they felt in that moment.

What happens is every time a conflict arises, and conflicts usually arise when people are talking about settlement terms, the person who was served by the sheriff mentally goes back to the time and place he or she was served with the divorce papers and becomes angry and resentful all over again. It is a distraction so great for many people that they cannot get beyond it enough to have the necessary conversations to divide the assets and liabilities or create a parenting plan.

People often think they need to file for divorce as soon as possible. They think it makes a difference if they, rather than their spouses, file first. They sometimes think that the person who files first is in the superior legal position. That is BS. In reality, filing for divorce creates a timeline and expense line over which you lose control unless you first speak to your spouse about who gets what assets and liabilities and what you are going to do with the kids. People who have divorced often tell stories about how they went to court, missed a day of work, spent $500 and nothing happened. That is BS.

Something did happen, just nothing that they understood and not anything that they believed got them closer to being divorced. Once a case in the court system, the legal system and its processes and procedures take over and to a large extent the litigants and even the lawyers lose control over the timeline and what happens when. The Judge, the representative of the Court, really wants a written, signed settlement agreement indicating how the parents intend to parent their children, how they will put their children through college and how they will divide the marital assets and debts and liabilities. Once the Husband and Wife sign a written settlement agreement and that agreement is approved by the Judge, the legal matter can be concluded, the Judge can close the file and the parties are divorced.

WHAT DO JUDGES WANT? TWO THINGS....

Divorce attorneys are litigators. They go to court every day. The primary reason a lawyer goes to court is to advise, update and tell the Judge how close or far apart the parties are to settlement. On those court days, if there is no written settlement agreement, the Judge will set the next court date, and instruct the lawyers on what the Judge wants for the next court date. The Judge requests things of the lawyers and the litigants which will move the parties and the case closer to a trial date.

Filing for divorce before having signed agreements jeopardizes your legal position and is unwise. It is BS. People save a lot of time in the court room when they wait to file for divorce. It is hard to have difficult, conflict-inducing discussions about money and children. It is harder to have them when the threat of pending legal action is hanging over everyone's head. Although, these conversations need to happen. Sometimes people confuse discussion and conversation with talking or communicating. Usually it is better not to talk but to continue to communicate.

COMMUNICATION COSTS

TRADITIONAL DIVORCE

6. Lawyer A calls Spouse A

5. Lawyer B calls Lawyer A

2. Lawyer A calls Lawyer B and position may be modified

5. Spouse B offers compromise to Lawyer B

3. Lawyer B calls Spouse B and postioning occurs

1. Spouse A calls Lawyer A

4. Spouse B thinks it over

7. Spouse A may get a distorted message

NO BS DIVORCE

4. Lawyer A and Lawyer B call respective clients

3. Lawyer A and Lawyer B engage in problem solving

2. Spouse A calls Lawyer A with questions or disputed issues

2. Spouse B calls Lawyer B with questions or disputed issues

1. Spouse A calls Spouse B (or texts, emails, meets with...)

1. Spouse B calls Spouse A (or texts, emails, meets with...)

When parties communicate information, which again does not necessarily mean talk, about the specifics of dividing the assets and liabilities and managing the children, they can resolve or at least reduce the number of their disputed issues. If they resolve their issues, they can file for divorce and complete the legal process in far less time than 18 months and likely within 90 days...or less. That is No BS.

Communication during the time the marriage is breaking down or has broken down is difficult. When divorcing, the primary reason to communicate is to transmit information about assets, liabilities and children.

Communication can be leaving a bank statement or credit card bill on the kitchen table in a place where the two people have agreed to exchange information. Each is free to process the information and make decisions about it without talking about it.

Here's an example:

Sheila and Sean could not talk to each other for more than ten minutes before one of them would start making derogatory comments about their in-laws. Although they tried to talk about what they would do with their house, they couldn't before the conversation deteriorated. There were a number of things to talk about, would they sell it, would one keep it, if they sold it, would they move before the children finished school, where would they move to, did they agree on the school district.

Rather than speak to each other, they set up a place in the kitchen where they put the divorce information. They agreed on who would do what. When Sean got the appraisal on the house, he put a copy for Sheila in the box. When Sheila found about the school district in the town she was thinking of moving to, she gave Sean a copy of the school information in the box. As each of them received the information, as can be imagined, they both blew up but not to or at each other. Both had the time they needed to think about the other's position. Although they didn't agree, they had what they needed to think about to settle the case. They also had the information that each of their lawyers needed without having to pay a lot of money to have subpoenas issued or experts hired.

Much of the banter about who did what to whom, why the divorce is happening, what each party did to the other and their in-laws was avoided. They spent their energy getting information related to the settlement agreement, to the needs of the children and to asset and liability division. The other conversations, which are irrelevant in most courtrooms and frequently the main cause of conflicts and difficulties were avoided.

I advise facing everything about a divorce as soon as possible.

The divorce, attorney-client relationship, therapy and other associated costs are expensive but manageable. Using an attorney wisely is great way to keep the financial resources in your family. When the attorney's time is used wisely, the client believes the money was well spent. Clients who know when to call the lawyer and when to call a friend will save money and make better decisions for themselves. Clients who have listened to their lawyer and who know the parameters of an equitable settlement for their matter, based on their facts, are less inclined to bicker needlessly over unrealistic positions. An equitable agreement is when the client gets a reasonable result, one to which he or she is legitimately entitled, and has avoided the expense of needless bickering.

Most good family law lawyers can achieve most of the reasonable requests and results for their clients. The range of options for settlement is very large and client goals can be accomplished in a number of creative ways. When clients want lawyers to advocate an unreasonable result, it can be very costly. Clients are best served when they take a few specific actions. Here are some suggestions:

Ask the lawyer predetermined questions during an initial consultation or interview. Here's *a secret*…going to a divorce attorney's office is very intimidating. Many people forget why they came, they don't know what to ask. They want the lawyer to like them so they will take their case. They also don't want to appear stupid. Write down your questions before you meet with the lawyer. Bring them to the meeting. The lawyer will tell you what you need to know about the process and the possible outcomes. We can't read your mind and don't know you, so ask your questions and let us tell you what you need to make good decisions. Ask any question relating to the lawyer's experience, availability, charges, hourly rate and staffing. Ask all questions about anything about the divorce that wakes you up at night. Ask the lawyer questions about their opinion of the best and worst case scenario given your facts. If you know who your spouse's lawyer is or the Judge who is assigned to your case, ask the lawyer how that might affect the outcome and the costs. Don't ask questions like "will I win?" "Will I lose?" but rather "What will I win?" "What will I lose?"

Remember winning and losing is relative to the person it is happening to. Our idea of winning and your idea of winning may be very different. "How long this will take? What it will cost? What can be done, what can I do, to keep the money in the family?" Ask how much it will cost to get the divorce given the results you want. Get the answers to your questions as soon as possible. If needed, seek out the advice of more than one attorney before you select your advocate. Most clients don't ask their real questions. That is BS.

When a lawyer quotes a "retainer," the client often misunderstands that to be the full cost of the divorce. It is not. It is only the initial amount required to "retain" the lawyer. In other words, it is the means to secure someone with an ethical obligation to act in their client's best interest and advocate the client's position. Paying a retainer ensures that that lawyer cannot represent the spouse. Paying a retainer ensures that someone has a legal representative to advocate for their wishes and move the case through the legal process, as long as the client continues to pay the agreed fees and hourly rate. The retainer is rarely the total amount paid.

It is a good idea to find out what the legal community in your area is charging for the services you are seeking. If you haven't asked the fee and costs questions, it is possible to decide to hire an attorney who requested less money up-front as a retainer. Verify why an initial retainer is less than the community norm. A reduced rate initial retainer could mean that the client may have to come up with more money sooner if the retainer is expended rapidly. In some cases, it could mean less client service, less attention to the file, more time to respond to client calls.

The old adage "you get what you pay for," although it generally applies in life, doesn't always apply with legal fees. Clients can be in for a surprise when they pay a reduced retainer rate and then are required to pay an additional retainer in a few weeks. As with other purchases, the "Buyer Beware" caution should be heeded.

Here are a few simple things to consider when hiring a divorce attorney:

Your advocate should be family law attorney who practices in the courthouse before the Judges who will have your case. Hire the divorce attorney who is versed in litigation, mediation, collaborative law and mental health evaluations. You want the best result for your life after the divorce. You are paying for the time it takes the attorney to get the job done but you are not paying for a specific result. The lawyers get paid for time, whether or not you win or lose your case. Hourly rates in your legal community will vary depending on an attorney's experience and success in their field. Hire a divorce lawyer who is skilled in family law and conflict resolution and fits within your budget.

Clients are usually billed at an hourly rate. Typically lawyers bill their time in increments of 10 or 15 minutes. The actual time, minutes and hours, is what the client pays for. This time is applied against the original retainer fee and additional retainers as paid. Lawyers will stop working on a case when the client has not paid his or her bill or owes the attorney money. The lawyer is the advocate in whom the client has invested a lot of time and money. That same lawyer may stop representing that client if the client owes more than the lawyer's business will tolerate. Some lawyers allow a client to carry a large unpaid balance, with the understanding that the fees will be paid out of other assets, such as a house, when the divorce is over. Other lawyers require the client to make payment in full each month. Still others require that the client account always has a set amount of money in it and they expect second, third and fourth retainers to be paid when each retainer is exhausted.

Fee issues, like all aspects of a divorce are best discussed in advance with the attorney. If the client has asked the questions about how they will be charged, what the full cost might be, when the lawyer may withdraw as a result of unpaid fees and the reality of what assets will be left or what debt will be created in the marital estate once the divorce is final, they will use their attorney time and money wisely.

There is a lot of BS surrounding the payment of and the amount charged as lawyers' fees. For example, it is a myth that you will not have to pay if your lawyer does not deliver a result. Actually, it is not a myth, it is BS. Clients pay for attorney time, not the results the attorney achieved or failed to achieve. As long as the attorney and the client have a contract which states the hourly rate, the client will be responsible for the payment of the bill for the lawyer's time. Clients who go to court to fight with their lawyers over the attorney fees they were charged often end up paying the reasonable and necessary fees the lawyer incurred for the case as well as those incurred for having to go to court to defend his or her bill.

Here are some of the things that take the lawyer's time that clients are billed for:

- Drafting or writing letters to opposing counsel or spouse if unrepresented
- Phone calls to or from you, including voice mail messages, often there is a minimum charge per phone call
- Cellular phone calls may be billed at a higher hourly rate
- Any time spent discussing your case or your phone calls with staff members
- Reading, reviewing, thinking about and answering e-mails
- Preparing the case strategy to get the result you are seeking
- Drafting pleadings, motions and court paperwork

- Communication, in any form, verbal, written, electronic, with opposing counsel regarding your matter
- Going to court for court appearances or filing of documents
- Travel and time for depositions and court.

Here are some of the terms in a typical retainer agreement:

1. There have been no representations or guarantees made by us regarding the outcome of this matter, as to the obtaining of a judgment or order for relief sought by you or your former spouse, as the case may be or as to the nature or amount of any awards, distributions or maintenance, child support, costs, the terms of any inter-spousal agreement or any other aspect of this matter.

2. Any discussions in this regard, past or present, are limited based upon our experience and judgment, the degree of cooperation between the two parties, the lawyers and the Judge.

3. This is only an estimate and should not be considered as a representation, promise or guarantee as to the result which might be obtainable, either in a contested trial or by way of a negotiated settlement.

Always, always, always understand that you are responsible for all fees due to your attorney. It is considered a marital expense in many jurisdictions and so if fees are paid by the marital estate from a joint checking account or a joint credit card, each of the parties has paid one half of the fees. As far as many family law attorneys are concerned, you, not your spouse are responsible for those fees. Yes, your spouse may be ordered to pay or contribute to your attorney fees. A Judge may also order that all fees be paid from a marital asset, like the proceeds from the sale of a house before the proceeds are distributed to either party. Don't mistakenly believe that your spouse will be responsible for payment of your attorney fees. To believe that your spouse will be required to pay your attorney's fees is BS.

Size up your divorce attorney in the initial interview. Make sure you like him or her because getting a divorce can be a long process and the possibility is that your attorney-client relationship could last 18 months or longer, it helps your process if you feel comfortable and confident working with them.

It is important that your attorney's "bedside manner" matches your personality and that you can see a good long-term working relationship. You will be divulging personal information and difficult emotional issues to your attorney. You will need to be candid about the result you want, the results you don't want, the actions you have taken which you will be accused of, the things you will be accused of that you did not do, what you can afford to pay and what you can't. Your new "best friend," your divorce lawyer, must be some-one you trust. You're paying for it...and that is No BS.

Tips for effectively using your billable attorney time.

Here are a few things to keep in mind that will help both you and your attorney keep your legal expenses within your budget:

- **Remember that attorney time is your money.** Ask how your attorney will bill for work on your case. Find out when your lawyer is on the clock and when he or she is not. Ask what they do and do not charge for.

- **Don't swamp your attorney with trivial details.** Your attorney is your legal advisor and needs regular communication from you. He or she may not need all the information you are providing and want to give. They will let you know what they need and when they need it.

- **Plan the frequency of communications with and the information provided to your attorney.** Keep a steno pad or the No BS Divorce Workbook handy and in a secure location so you can keep a current list of items, questions and concerns you think you need to discuss with your lawyer. These questions and concerns will arise at any time and any place. Keeping the information in one place helps to organize your thoughts and information. This is true especially as you are considering settlement options. You will forget what you have been told. Being able to refer back to it may save you a phone call or two to your attorney.

- **When you have decided how frequently you need to communicate with your lawyer, call them, once a week or once a month, whatever works for you.** Schedule a phone conference time with your lawyer to discuss your current list of questions. Scheduling a set time to talk to your lawyer assures that your lawyer is available when you call and your lawyer can dedicate that time to your call and your questions. Calling your lawyer every day or whenever a non-major event occurs and expecting your lawyer to take immediate action will only frustrate you because it is unlikely your attorney will be available to take your call. Most divorce lawyers' days and schedules follow a very predictable path. That path is detailed later in this chapter.

- **Your lawyer is your legal representative, not your psychologist or your mental health advisor.** Lawyers are trained in legal problem solving. Although lawyers who practice family law are very good at dealing with emotional and psychological issues, clients are better served when they pay a mental health professional for help with mental and emotional challenges. Remember that you're paying for your attorney's time. If you want to call us because you need a shoulder to cry on, that's OK. However, your money and resources may be more wisely spent if you contact your church, call a good friend or relative or make an appointment with a mental health professional. Each of these routes is usually cheaper, faster and more effective.

- **Take the time to make an informed decision about choosing a lawyer.** It will be time well spent. You will be more likely to pick someone who will match your needs and deliver results that will sustain the test of time...in other words, keep you out of the courthouse for years to come

- **Once you picked your lawyer, then you have to figure how you can best work together.** From a fee stand point, the more work you do for your lawyer, the less work your lawyer will have to do for you and the less it may cost you. Be your own legal assistant. When your attorney requests information or documents from you, provide what they ask for, in the manner they ask it to be provided, when they request it. If your lawyer requests multiple copies of documents, take them to a copy shop and do it yourself. Organize and index documents before giving them to your attorney. This will save your lawyer time and save you money. That is No BS

- **When you are asked by your attorney to produce documents, such as bank statement, loan documents, credit card statements, tax returns, make three copies: one for your lawyer, one for the Judge and one for your spouse's attorney, the opposing counsel.** You will keep the originals. At some point, you may be asked to produce the original documents, but copies will frequently suffice most of the time. Of course, you could have the lawyer or their staff make copies for you, but you will be charged for the time and the copies.

- **Be willing to compromise within the range of your best case scenarios.** Be creative, flexible and come up with many options to settle your case as you can think of. There is no one way to settle your divorce case. Give thought to how you could resolve the disputed issues regarding the children, assets and liabilities. The exact same facts may result in a very different settlement because of the parties, the lawyers or the Judge. That is No BS. The more amicable or professional the conduct between the spouses, the more likely the parties will create their own settlement, the more likely the matter can be resolved quickly and cost effectively, the more likely the children will be less traumatized and the more likely the parties will retain their financial resources in both parties' pockets.

- **Consider alternatives to litigation to end disputes.** Processes that facilitate conflict resolution include divorce mediation and collaborative divorce. Try to resolve your differences in the most effective manner which is usually the least hostile way. In addition to spending less on legal fees, you will model problem-solving skills which will be passed on to your children.

- **Be clear about your objectives for settlement and the strategies you want to take to get a settlement you can live with.** When divorce attorneys give advice to clients, the advice is only as good as the information those clients provide. Sometimes clients fail to disclose important information which might dramatically change the possible outcomes. That omission makes a difference in the advice the lawyer might give. Inaccurate or insufficient information can also hinder the success of a particular legal position. If a lawyer has to invoke the legal system to learn facts that could have been accurately stated by a client, but weren't, it often causes the costs of a divorce case to increase. The more accurately clients detail their case and provide an accurate assessment of the facts, the better the advice and strategy they will receive from their lawyers.

- **One phone call, one e-mail or one letter to most lawyers is sufficient.** There is no need to call multiple times during the day or the week. Besides delaying the lawyer's ability to return your call or respond to your e-mail, multiple calls are billed to your account. When you do call the lawyer's office and are not able to reach your attorney, leave a detailed message with staff or on the attorney's voice mail. Make it easy for the attorney to return your call when he or she can. Leave a phone number where you can be reached and a good time to return the call. If you don't leave a phone number, the attorney cannot return your call until he or she returns to the office or finds your phone number. Most of us call our offices for messages when we are in court.

When we retrieve messages, we typically return the easy calls, the ones we can act on in the amount of time we have. When your attorney is in court, he or she is fairly unreachable. There is often some break in the schedule that allows the lawyer to make quick phone calls. If we are in court, we know we may have to end the conversation quickly if we get called back into the court room. Most attorneys return calls that they think can be addressed and finished quickly. We know which clients will keep us on the phone longer than the time we have. We are reluctant to call clients during our courtroom break when we believe they will keep us on the phone a long time or longer than the time we have at that moment. And attorneys call the clients they like to talk to... that is No BS.

- **Plan and think in one week increments.** Many people going through a divorce find this concept hard to grasp. This is how many divorce lawyers plan their schedule for the week. We schedule our work flow and we prioritize our work load in weekly segments. Once the schedule is set, it is harder for the client to get the response they want and harder for us to do what we want to do for each client. The more time clients give lawyers to take action or return a call, the more successfully the lawyer can represent the clients and give them what they want without crisis. This is true because the lawyer can respond rather than react to the client matter.

Here's what a typical divorce lawyer's day looks like:

LAWYER'S TYPICAL DAY

TODAY!

6
7 _Meet with paralegal at office_
8 _Court - 8:15_
9 _- attending to_
10 _client court matters -_
11
12 _Bar Association commitee meeting_
1 _Check in w office staff. Client A Meeting_
2 _Client B meeting_
3 _Client C meeting_
4 _Trial preparation_
5
6 _Possible new Client C consultation_

Money Matters

In addition to attorney fees, another money matter to consider is how your day-to-day expenses will be handled while the divorce is pending as well as after the divorce has been finalized. Clients often have not thought about their own personal money management style. One of the more difficult things to talk about is how the bills are going to be paid while the marriage is breaking down. To ensure some financial security, clients often have to re-evaluate their ability to manage finances and pay household bills. In a marriage, one person is typically responsible for the money issues, while the other is typically responsible for the day-to-day household management. When a family is in the midst of a divorce, both parties have to be fully apprised of the financial situation of the marriage so they can make informed decisions about their financial future and so they can intelligently enter into a settlement agreement that they will be satisfied with. This information is crucial when parties want to make good financial decisions and finalize settlement terms so they can finalize the divorce.

On the following pages, you'll see what happens to a family's resources before, during and after a divorce using both the traditional divorce model and the No BS divorce model.

Even when both spouses are working during the breakdown of the marriage, family income and expenses are likely to change and the family budget will fluctuate accordingly. Financial matters are included in settlement negotiations and the final settlement documents include paying or receiving child support, support for a spouse, sometimes called maintenance—sometimes called alimony, health care costs for yourself and your children, therapy, the costs associated with children's activities, car insurance for the children, college expenses and any other expenses both parents want for themselves and their children.

Here are some things to consider to keep your money in your family:

- **Avoid using joint charge cards.** Don't start spending money generally or on credit cards just to get even with your spouse because they want a divorce. Remember that if accounts are jointly held, both parties will likely be responsible for paying off the balance. Don't run up more debt than you want to be responsible for.

- **Don't take out any new joint loans or open credit card accounts with your spouse.** You may be responsible for those balances as well.

- **Save money whenever and wherever you can.** There are many expenses involved when people are separating. These expenses may include the costs of moving, the costs of the second residence, new furniture for both residences, personal property items, cost of therapy and post-judgment legal fees for any unfinished work, such as division of retirement assets. When couples manage the expense of a divorce and keep it within their budget, they will save the family's financial resources. Those savings translate into dollars in your pocket and may mean that you will be financially better able to begin your life after divorce with some assets rather than some liabilities.

- **Set a definite date with your spouse for when you will close or stop using joint accounts.** Send a letter, perhaps certified, to the credit card companies you are using or keeping. Request a new credit card in your name only. The Equal Credit Opportunity Act requires credit card companies to grant you a credit card with a credit limit equal to that of your current card.

- **Pay all utilities on time, especially if they are in your name.** If you have not been a good paying customer in the past, you may be asked to pay a security deposit when you establish a new account. This is also true for rent and mortgage payments. Many landlords will check your credit. If your payment history is poor, you may have to make higher deposits or you may be denied entirely.

- **Investigate which bills you don't have now that you will have in the future and which bills you have now you won't have in the future because of different living arrangements.** Make these decision based upon what you can reasonably afford with your post-divorce income and assets. Plan conservatively. Although you may be receiving child support or spousal support, don't depend on those payments when making decisions for future expenditures.

- **Make copies of all financial and tax records for each spouse so that each will have their own copies after the divorce.** These records may be necessary for future tax returns or audits and no one wants to give old records to their former spouse. Do it before the divorce is finalized.

- **If estimated taxes have been paid prior to the divorce and a tax refund or tax liability is expected, make a decision before the divorce is finalized about how the refund will be handled and much each party will get.**

- **Don't spend thousands of dollars in attorney fees fighting over a $150 piece of furniture.** Use common sense and simple math when deciding what you want to fight for and at what cost you should fight for it.

- **Don't be foolish. Don't be greedy. Pick your battles.** It doesn't matter who wanted the divorce or why. That is No BS... even although people often think these things do matter. Even when your emotions are running high and even when you may be the "wronged" spouse, you won't get more than the law in your state provides. Find out what you're entitled to in your state and that is No BS.

IMPACT ON FAMILY RESOURCES

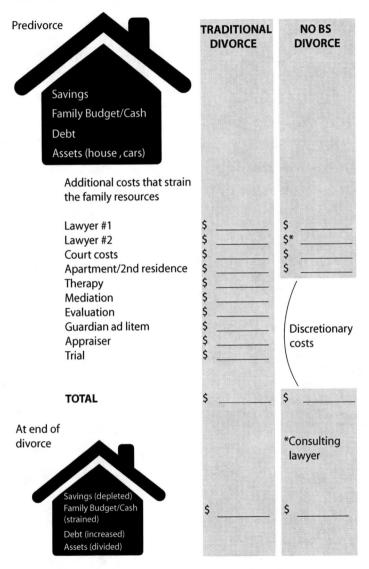

Predivorce

Savings
Family Budget/Cash
Debt
Assets (house , cars)

	TRADITIONAL DIVORCE	NO BS DIVORCE
Additional costs that strain the family resources		
Lawyer #1	$ _____	$ _____
Lawyer #2	$ _____	$* _____
Court costs	$ _____	$ _____
Apartment/2nd residence	$ _____	$ _____
Therapy	$ _____	
Mediation	$ _____	
Evaluation	$ _____	
Guardian ad litem	$ _____	Discretionary costs
Appraiser	$ _____	
Trial	$ _____	
TOTAL	$ _____	$ _____

At end of divorce

*Consulting lawyer

Savings (depleted)
Family Budget/Cash (strained)
Debt (increased)
Assets (divided)

$ _____ $ _____

Chapter Three:
The Reality...Myths and Misconceptions that Could Cost You

Family Myths (that are Mostly BS)

1. **Love is everlasting.** That is BS. If that were true, people would stay married 'til death did part them and they would not need to get divorced.

2. **You will never see your kids again.** That is BS. It is very difficult to take children away from their natural parent. The court system honors parents' rights and, except in some very dangerous or harmful situations, the Judge is reluctant to prevent any parent from getting access to their children or preventing any child from having a relationship with a parent, no matter how few parenting skills they may have. The Judge may even require a parent to take their children to a jail to visit a convicted parent so that the children have some relationship with them.

3. **I (your spouse) am going to take you to Court for everything you are worth** - resources, legacies, children, etc. and make sure the Judge gives you nothing. That is BS. People may decide to walk away from all their assets because the pressure to fight for

them is too great. They may also do so when they are so desperate to end the marriage. But the Judge will divide resources equitably and fairly, although your vision of what is fair and the Judge's vision of what is fair may be completely different. Of course, if the combined costs of the divorce, therapy, appraisals, attorney fees and the legal process have depleted the marital assets and there are no resources left at the end of the process, then the Judge will have nothing to divide. Many people think that a Judge can make a person give back an asset or pay for an asset that no longer exists. That is BS. A Judge can only divide the assets and liabilities that exist on the date when the matter is brought before him or her...potentially 18 months after the divorce was filed. During those 18 months, most divorcing families have incurred additional expenses of setting up two households, hiring two lawyers and scheduling additional therapy, among other things. There may be nothing more than debt to divide between the two people. That is No BS.

4. **My spouse (or I) will be fair.** That is usually BS. "Fair" is a very relative and subjective term. One of Oxford's definitions of fair is "moderately good"; another is "just or appropriate in the circumstances." My idea of fair, your idea of fair, your spouse's idea of fair, your Mother's idea of fair, your best friend's idea of fair, your lawyer's idea of fair, your

spouse's lawyer's idea of fair and the Judge's idea of fair may not be the same at all. In addition, the longer it takes to settle the case, the more likely ideas of fairness change. What someone thinks is fair at the time they are contemplating a divorce is usually very different at the time they are signing settlement documents. What a spouse thinks is fair and is willing to do when the financial resources are all in tact and what a spouse thinks is fair or what they can realistically do once the financial resources have been depleted may result in two very different settlement agreements.

5. **You don't need a lawyer.** We don't need two lawyers. That is BS. And I'm not saying that it is BS because I'm a lawyer or because I love lawyers or because I believe everyone should have a lawyer. People need to be smart about using lawyers, especially when they are getting a divorce. Lawyers are ethically bound to their clients and cannot serve two masters. Even if people only want to "use one lawyer," the lawyer can't do it—a lawyer cannot represent both divorcing spouses. Lawyers will always advise the party they are not representing to consult with another lawyer before signing any legal documents, especiallymarital settlement agreements. Many lawyers won't talk to the spouse of their client. In some instances, if they do speak with the spouse, they let the spouse know, in writing, that they are

not representing them. In many cases, retaining two lawyers may be unnecessary, but each person should consult with an independent lawyer before signing any documents related to a divorce. That is No BS.

6. **My lawyer told me that I can drag this out by having all your friends come to court to say how bad you really are.** That is BS. In reality, about 97% of all divorce cases settle and only about 3% of divorce cases actually go in front of a Judge for a trial. Even if Judges had the time, which they don't, they are very smart people. They do not need to have fifteen witnesses tell them the same thing and they do not have the time, the desire or the need to listen to days of testimony about divorce issues. Most of the issues the Judge needs testimony about are usually related to your family finances and how they should be divided. Most friends can't testify to those issues. Judges don't need to hear the same testimony by multiple persons because it's redundant, unnecessary and a waste of the Judges' time. And, even if they do, which they don't, you would have the same opportunity to present your witness to rebut any negative testimony your spouse's witnesses may have provided. That is No BS.

7. **The Judge is going to see the truth of what a bad person and bad parent you are and will punish**

you and you will never be able to do that again.
That is BS. The court does not regulate marital behavior or parenting style. Although Judges strive
to protect children and make decisions that are in
the "best interest of the child," Judges cannot po-
lice or monitor the parents' behavior. That is No BS.
But, although that is No BS, your spouse could still
make life more difficult for you if he or she is trying
to punish you, just because.

8. **This will all be over at our next court date.** Or, this
will all be over before you know what hit you. That
is BS. The slowest person (the person not ready to be
divorced) controls the timeline. Judges will give parties a limited amount of time to process the impact
of the divorce and to hire lawyers, answer pleadings
and participate in the legal process. It is difficult for
anything to happen in a courtroom without a party's
knowledge because there are rules about how and
when someone must be notified of any court action.

In the case where something happens in a spouse's
absence, most jurisdictions have procedural rules
which will allow someone thirty days to vacate any
court orders that the Judge has signed and entered.
The only time the case will be over "on the next
court date" or "before you know what hit you" is
if you are not participating in the process and are
defaulted for failure to participate or when all the

paperwork is signed and ready to be entered or if the next court date is a trial date. That is No BS.

9. **Once I file for divorce, the Judge will kick my spouse out of the house.** That is BS. In truth, Judges are reluctant to remove people from their homes. This reluctance is due to many reasons, including the economic impact of setting up a second household, depleting family resources faster and wanting to preserve assets for each of you and, more importantly, the children. Absent serious abuse or domestic violence, Husbands and Wives usually have to live together, in a pressure cooker, until the divorce is finalized. That is No BS.

10. **I will get the kids because I am the better parent.** That is BS. Most Judges believe that except in very rare circumstances, it is in children's best interest to have adequate access to both parents despite their strengths and weaknesses as parents. Except in situations involving serious abuse, usually physical abuse, Judges do not take children away from their natural parents. That is No BS.

11. **My spouse must stay within five miles of my house so I can see my kids.** That is BS. Most of you reading this book live in America. In America, no non-criminal court can require any spouse to live or to stay anywhere, especially not with-

in a geographically limited area, near another spouse. They can however, limit where the children live, usually within the confines of the state where the divorce is occurring. Parents can agree that they will live within a certain area and if in the settlement documents, the Judge can enforce it. Both parties have to decide what makes sense as they contemplate their separation and consider the reality of their particular circumstance.

For some, a move is predictable because during the marriage moves occurred every three years. For others a job change and relocation could mean a potential move. In some jurisdictions, the Judge has authority to limit where the children move and may require the children to stay in the state where the divorce occurred. As our society becomes increasingly mobile, the question of the likelihood of your or your spouse or your children moving out of state becomes an excellent initial question for your lawyer...and that is No BS.

12. **The kids aren't affected by the divorce; they don't even know it's happening.** That is BS. Most children are affected because most parents cannot hide their pain and many parents knowingly or unwittingly involve their children in their pain. It is foolish to think that children do not see the pain in the two people they love most in the world. The

children tune into the fights and the discussions. They listen to a Mother's conversation with her best friend or a Father's conversation with his parents. They want to know what is going on because they are scared. They do not have the life experience to manage the divorce. Often, their parents don't either. The effects are not only short term.

Because the parents are the primary role model for their children, how they handle their divorce is what their children learn. If parents are constantly in court, years later the likelihood of their children getting divorced is great. Their children who are affected by the divorce will be our future clients and the court's the next litigants. That is No BS.

13. **My girlfriend/best friend/sister got "everything" in her divorce so I will too…**[see #3 and #4]. Every divorce case is different. There are reasons why someone might get everything in their divorce. Someone who is desperate to get out of the marriage may agree to settlement documents which provide that they walk away with no assets and a lot of debt or with less than to what they are entitled. Those cases are few and far between but occur when someone just has to be done, for whatever reason. Just because your girlfriend/best friend/sister got everything does not mean you will. That is No BS.

14. **My spouse will use the fact that I take medication (or that I am in a twelve-step program of recovery) against me and will take the kids away from me.** That is BS. Spouses may and do threaten to do that to try to get a leg up or to try to manipulate their spouse who does not want the information exposed. But the good news is that Judges like people who recognize that they have a problem and then get the help they need. Getting that help often makes it very easy for a Judge to decide that the recovering/medicated parent is better able to see a problem and address it. That is No BS.

15. **Once I get divorced, I will never have to speak to him/her again.** That depends. This statement is probably true if there are no children involved. If there are children however, it is BS. When you have children together, you will have to speak to your ex-spouse again and perhaps regularly. The Mother-Father relationship and the need to communicate and cooperate to act in the children's best interest is never over, even when the children are adults. Parenting time schedules, vacations, day-to-day activities and important events like graduations have to be coordinated.

Keeping your divorced relationship businesslike, respectful and when possible, amicable as it relates to communication about the children will make your lives easier and the situation more comfortable and acceptable for your children. That is No BS.

16. **I can avoid hiring or consulting with a lawyer if I use the internet or the law library.** I am smart and resourceful. I can find paperwork, write it up and get the divorce done. That is almost always BS. The internet and law library are excellent resources to start gathering the information you need to get a divorce. Many people try to use the internet and law libraries to do their own divorce. Some have done it very successfully, others have found that they unintentionally gave away large assets to their spouse. Searching the internet and doing your own divorce may not be the wisest decision for a variety of reasons. Internet documents may not address all the children, assets or liability issues of your marriage.

Once the divorce has been finalized, if you missed something, it is very difficult to have a Judge reopen a closed divorce. Second, if the documents fail to address an important issue, the Judge assigned to your case cannot save you from a bad deal that you and your spouse create. It is not the Judge's job to give you advice about your settlement terms. Judges only determine if the deal you present to him to sign is reasonable according to the laws within the state or jurisdiction in which you bring your case. You might give away assets that a Judge knows is happening but cannot stop you from doing. Here is a really interesting reminder: *Anyone who is his own lawyer has a fool for a client.*

17. **The kids will decide which parent they want to live with and where they will live.** That is BS. Parents should never put children in the position or situation where they are forced to choose between two parents. It is an adult decision to be made by adults. If the parents cannot make it, the Judges will. Judges and lawyers do not like to put the immense burden of that decision on a minor. In addition to the fact that they don't have the life experience to make the decision, we can't always know their motive for wanting to live with one parent over another. We can suspect the level of discipline in a house may have something to do with it as well as a host of other motives. Parents often give that decision-making power to their minor children, but Judges won't. That is No BS.

18. **Once the divorce is over, we'll all get along great and things will all be okay.** That might be BS. The ability to get along after a divorce really depends upon the two people, the emotional (and sometimes financial) damage done during the process, how committed the two of them are to setting aside their differences to successfully raise their children and what conflict resolution skills both parties have.

Getting along, great or otherwise, after a divorce is finalized will not happen unless both parties are committed to setting aside their differences, having a business-like relationship and parenting the children successfully...whatever that looks like for them. That is No BS.

BS Busters— I'd like to say it's BS, but . . . it's not

1. **I went to court today, it cost me $500 and nothing happened.** This is really not true. Something always happens in court, but that "something" is often not what you thought would happen or perhaps secretly hoped for. Every court date has a purpose. The purpose may be to advise the Judge of the status of the settlement negotiations, it may be to order the next legal procedure to prepare the case for trial, it may be to decide how long the trial will take. Only about 3% of cases go to trial, so although the court procedure has a purpose, clients generally do not perceive much of the required work done in the court as serving a good purpose, which for them is to get the divorce finalized. Something always happens at court, it is almost always procedural, it just isn't always what the client hoped for.

2. **We are getting a divorce and I don't have to talk to my spouse.** If you want to resolve your differences

and get the divorce finished, you must communicate with your spouse. If you don't communicate what terms you want in the settlement documents, it will take longer to finish the divorce. However, you don't have to necessarily talk with or speak to your spouse.

One of the easiest ways to communicate settlement terms is in writing, either by e-mail or letter. Writing is a better form of communication for a variety of reasons. First, both parties have controlled responses. Unless someone just blasts off an angry letter, the writer will be more tempered in what he or she communicates, they will read it, sleep on it and reread and edit it before they actually send it. When the recipient gets the written communication, they can control when and where they read it. They can have their emotional "blow up" away from the presence of the writer. They will have time to cool off and respond in a less emotional manner. Both parties have presented their sides without giving the other additional emotional leverage against them.

3. **I will drag this out and make your life miserable.** This is true. One party often does not want the divorce. That person can control how quickly or how slowly the process moves along. Our clients come in various emotional states. Some like the quick, intense pain and want it over and some like the

long, painful, dull, nagging and continual pain and don't want it over too fast. The Court process will move on a schedule interrupted by continuances and delays. Prolonging a resolution, delaying getting on with life or starting a new one and perhaps making life miserable may also have monetary consequences. Consider this statement: The faster you get the divorce done, the sooner the pain is over, the more financial resources you will have and the sooner you can begin to live your new life...even if it was not the life you dreamed about.

4. **I will tell the kids what a bad person you are.** This is true. People say and do stupid things when it comes to their children...especially when they are in pain, when their hopes and dreams are being dashed and shattered and when they feel completely powerless. Parents frequently tell their children too much information about their life, the other parent and the divorce. Under the guise of thinking the children need to know what is happening, people often tell the children a one-sided version of the truth. The children often have limited ability to filter out the real from the unreal. If people can keep the children out of the divorce discussion and if they assure the children that the adults will work it out, the children will do better in life. That is No BS.

5. **I'm only going to do what my lawyer tells me to do**

and he said not to talk to you, so I won't talk to you about anything, including the settlement terms. This is often true. Clients often become fearful to take any action without their lawyer's input and approval. They are paralyzed and unable to make decisions that under normal circumstances they really are fully capable of making on their own, without legal counsel. We lawyers won't live with the consequences of your decisions or your actions. Our lives won't be altered if you decide not to follow the legal advice you're paying for. They won't be altered if you decide to follow the legal advice we give. The consequences of your actions merely determine the legal path we will take to close your case. When the client only does what their lawyer tells them to do, the divorce may take even longer to get done.

Chapter Four:
Setting Your Divorce Timeline...
When to Decide What

When the decision to get a divorce has been made, establishing a realistic timeline and deciding when it will be finalized seems like an idealistic approach. But when people take charge of their timelines, they make better decisions and they can better plan their lives.

TRADITIONAL DIVORCE

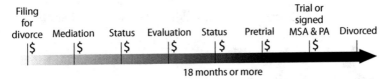

No BS DIVORCE

Here is an example:

In March, Eileen was desperate to get Shamus out of the house. She thought she could buy out his interest in the house. Their daughter was graduating from high school in three months. Eileen wanted to spend her energy enjoying her daughter's senior year. She did not want to spend a lot of time dealing with the things that had to be done to get the divorce before the graduation. She and Shamus were not communicating. Eileen wanted to be divorced after Kelly's graduation party. She wanted Shamus to be a part of the graduation plans but from a distance. She knew until she could buy him out, Shamus was not leaving.

In this instance, Eileen got the information from her lawyer about what she needed to finalize the divorce. She set up a meeting with Shamus at their local coffee shop. She let him know the meeting would last one hour and there were five things she needed to talk to him about.

They met a week later and Eileen laid out the plan of action. She told him she wanted to him to be out of the house by September 1 or as soon as their daughter went off to college. She told him she would pay him $30,000 for his interest in the house on the day he moved out. She told him she wanted him to be at the graduation party and that she did not want his family or her family excluded from the party but that she would only be comfortable with his family present if they did not know of the pending divorce. But if they did know about the divorce, they could come but could not talk to her or Kelly about it. She told him she wanted to be divorced by their twenty-third wedding anniversary.

What happened?

This seemingly typical scenario is not a simple example. First, it is very difficult to decide to have a meeting with a spouse and it is harder to talk about these issues. Each one of the issues in the example will impact whether or not Eileen can be divorced by her twenty-third anniversary. Each one affects her ideal timeline and each affects her Husband's ideal timeline.

But here's how Eileen controlled the timeline. First, she met with her lawyer. Second, she decided when she wanted to be divorced. Third, she clearly told Shamus her position and by doing so limited his ability to communicate to her about things that didn't have any impact on the final resolution. Of course, Shamus had his own ideas which he communicated to Eileen. Because she set the stage for the discussion, Shamus, although not in agreement with everything Eileen wanted, was able to propose some very specific suggestions that made sense for the family. Because Eileen knew what her ultimate goal was, she was able to compromise on the things that were not as important to her.

Sounds easy. It would be if you were dealing with your best friend or a co-worker. It is not easy when you have to do it with a spouse. It is not easy when additional players are involved, like your lawyer, your spouse's lawyer, your family and friends, his family and friends and of course, the Judge.

Here are some decisions that have to be made that may impact the timeline for finalizing a divorce.

1. **Selling a house or having a house sit on the market.** A Husband and Wife may not be financially

able to physically separate until a house is sold and the proceeds divided between them. The financial climate of the time and the geographic area in which a family lives could mean the house may sit on the market for a while. Decisions about who stays in the house, who moves, who pays the bills and who does the maintenance all have to be made.

2. **The need for and the ability to get health insurance.** Securing individual health insurance coverage for the dependent spouse may affect the timeline. If both parties have their own medical insurance coverage before the divorce is finalized, it is not an issue which could determine the divorce date. If the dependent spouse elects COBRA coverage, it is not an issue regarding the timeline. The divorce timeline could be affected when the dependent spouse needs to secure independent coverage and when the proposed insurer has a required waiting period or if one party has a pre-existing medical condition.

3. **The income tax considerations.** The date selected to finalize a divorce may be determined by whether parties want to file joint or separate tax returns. If the goal is keeping money in the family and if the tax implications of filing a joint return are better for the family, then waiting to finalize the divorce until after December 31 is a must. You have to be

married on December 31 of the tax year in order to file a joint tax return with your soon-to-be-former spouse. It may not make any difference in how much you pay if you were divorced and were required to file separately, but it is a question to be considered when selecting your date of divorce.

Here are some suggested questions to ask when you reach an impasse in the meeting. Sometimes changing the subject for a few minutes makes it easier to get back to the tasks at hand. Many can be used to overcome an impasse.

- What is your ideal picture of what life will look like once a divorce is final?
- Will we attend family functions together?
- How will that work?
- Will we share the children's birthdays?
- How close will we live to each other?
- What will we say if we see each other in the grocery store?
- How will we behave when we meet unexpectedly?

Using questions such as these to talk about and perhaps explore what life may be like in the future often helps take the focus off the immediate problem and may even eliminate those uncomfortable situations that will arise during the breakdown of the marriage and after the divorce is final.

The most obvious impediment to getting the divorce done by or on a certain date is whether or not your spouse has the desire or the ability to get the divorce finalized by that target date. If you want to have the divorce finished by a certain date, your approach to your spouse has to be in a way that they will respond positively, not negatively to your suggestion. If your spouse is just not ready to be divorced, having regular, ongoing discussions helps to get them ready for the inevitable. Making the fact that the divorce is a reality and not sending mixed messages about that reality will make reaching a successful resolution on your timeline possible. Your patience and your frustration levels with your spouse will impact their ability to process the information and impact how quickly or how slowly your spouse will act on your requests.

Finally, *the big secret* to getting a divorce on a manageable timeline is having effective communication with your spouse. I often say to clients: "When my Husband tells me something, frequently my first reaction is 'I don't think so.'" It doesn't matter what he tells me, it could be important, it could be trivial, it is just my automatic response to him. My best girlfriend can tell me the exact same thing and I will think she is a genius. Unfair? Absolutely. But I am not unique in that. The fact that I am aware that I automatically react to him because he sent the information and that, most of the time, I am not reacting to the information itself, keeps me from saying or doing something I will regret later. I have found that for people who are divorcing, this is especially true. They not only don't want to listen to anything coming from their spouse but they also have a bad reaction to everything they say! *Secret,* you don't have to like what your spouse has to say and you don't have to like your spouse, but it is a good idea to pay attention to what they say because you may find it in a settlement document and have to respond to it anyway.

In most jurisdictions, when spouses make these informal agreements outside of the courtroom, they are not binding. Spouses make all types of agreements and may or may not follow through with them…just like in a marriage. When discussing settlement terms with your spouse be aware that no decision is final and nothing is legally agreed upon, even if you and your spouse say it's agreed, until a Judge says it's agreed and it's final—and even then there are some exceptions. Both parties have a lot of freedom and flexibility to be creative in figuring out options for settlement. They have the ability communicate without risk of legal consequences. An agreement between spouses becomes binding on both when it is reduced to writing, approved by the lawyers, signed by both parties AND signed by a Judge. Sometimes, parties are close to final agreement. So close that they have signed papers and are presenting them to a Judge. If in that moment, one of the parties decides they don't want to be bound to that agreement, a Judge may decide not to approve an agreement. It can happen on the final day of court, when one party tells the Judge they have changed their mind and they no longer agree to the proposed settlement terms. There are a lot of reasons why this might happen. One, the person is really not ready to be divorced and the finality of it is just too much for them to process or cope with. Two, one spouse has talked to someone who gave him or her the perfect reason why they should not agree to the terms that had previously perceived as a good idea. Three, "Just because!"

Those many agreements between spouses will be considered tentatively in place until all parts of the total settlement agreement have been considered. Those parts include children, assets and liabilities. Divorcing couples should make agreements, lots of them, because there are a lot of things to be decided. However, know that spouses can change their minds on several issues and several issues may be tied to issues that have not been discussed or decided.

Here are some suggestions about how and what to do get an agreement done:

First, plan for success. If possible, plan to meet your spouse on neutral ground, at a neutral time. The meeting can be at your local coffee shop, a library or a friend's home. Meeting in your home, or if you have already separated in either of your homes, is not neutral. Each of you should arrive and depart separately. Take separate cars. This creates the ability for either of you to leave. If the discussion gets heated, (although if you picked a neutral ground most discussions don't get too heated), and one of you just has to leave, each of you will have a get away car as part of your exit strategy. This exit strategy ensures that neither of you will be trapped in a car with an angry spouse and will give each of you the space needed to process the difficult conversations.

Second, know each of your time tolerances, that is, how long can you be together and talk civilly to each other. If the two of you can sit and talk successfully for thirty minutes, do not try for thirty-one minutes. If it is sixty minutes, do not try for sixty-one...even if you are making progress. If one of you can meet and talk for twenty minutes and the other can meet and talk for three hours, meet and talk for twenty minutes. You will frequently have success. In my experience, when people are together for more time than one of them can tolerate, at some point the conversation and the discussion will start to deteriorate and often undo the good work that they were able to do within their time tolerance. It doesn't matter who has the least amount of tolerance or why. Schedule the amount of time that both parties can tolerate...even if that means several meetings for short periods of time.

Third, before the actual meeting, decide what the topics of discussion will include on that particular date for that amount of time, an agenda. Do not deviate from the planned agenda unless there is a pressing family matter that came up and needs the immediate attention of both of you and that you both want to talk about. Routine, day-to-day items will come up that will not be on the agenda that will need to be discussed. Defer those items to a different day. Having more meetings for shorter periods of time is frequently the key to successfully chipping away at all the topics which need to be discussed so that the divorce can be concluded. Sometimes, documents will be needed to be able to have productive discussions. An agenda item might be what information and documents needs to be exchanged, what needs to be supplemented and what needs to be appraised and when will that occur.

Fourth, take stock and inventory your immediate concerns. They could be emotional, financial, medical or physical. These concerns will frequently overshadow the ability to make long-range settlement decisions and may need to be adjusted as the family budget changes. Be prepared to postpone other items on the agenda because of a pressing issue which arose. For example, the transmission on the car went out, should it be repaired or should a new car be purchased. Address the pressing concerns when they need to be addressed. Putting off those difficult conversations frequently makes a small but pressing issue into a larger and more pressing one. These pressing concerns may involve the children and their care, the payment of household bills, living arrangements, etc.

It is BS to think that you don't need to communicate with your spouse because one of you decided to get a divorce. Figuring out how to communicate while you are going through the divorce is great practice for being able to communicate once the divorce is finalized. It is better to learn your real time tolerance to be with your spouse, making mistakes while you are moving toward separation and divorce. It is really difficult to learn that once you are divorced. Mistakes, like these will serve as valuable lessons that will help both parties communicate more effectively when they are living in two separate households.

Finally, think about how you want to handle the areas that you know you and your spouse disagree about before you go to the meeting. It is those disputes that create impasses in the meeting. When you have a disputed item on the agenda or reach an impasse (and you will reach an impasse), decide whether you will continue the meeting and discuss other items on the agenda or if you will cancel the meeting until the next planned date. Impasses over the division of property or the children's schedules are not "dead ends."

Dividing assets and debts is a process which occurs over the course of several meetings. Between meetings, one or both of the spouses may change their position and perhaps their priorities about the assets. At one meeting they may be willing to let the other spouse have something and the next one, not as willing. Sometimes, upon further reflection, both spouses realize that neither can afford to keep a certain asset and that the best plan is to sell it. Time can be a valuable ally that can work to your benefit if you are not prematurely involved in litigation. Once an impasse is reached, it is often wise to table a discussion regarding assets until a subsequent session.

When continuing to try to resolve a truly disputed issue would not be productive, it is perfectly acceptable to save that issue for the end of the process or defer the issue to the lawyers. Remember, it is better to reduce the number of disputed issues you need your lawyer to handle and concentrate on the areas and issues that you and your spouse can or already do agree on.

Here are some sample agreements that spouses often

make before the divorce is finalized. Many of these reduce day-to-day conflict between spouses.

- The parents agree not to question or try to get information from the children about the other parent both during and after the divorce.
- The parents agree not to question the children about the other parent's personal life, activities they are involved in or individuals they go to dinner with.
- The parents agree the children may have their friends over and in the house between 3 pm and 6 pm even if a parent is not home.
- The parents agree that Mom will be responsible for the children during the week and Dad will be responsible for the children during the weekend.
- The parties agree the household chores will be divided as follows. Mom will be responsible for certain tasks (cleaning up the bedrooms, pick up, laundry, meals during the week), Dad will be responsible for other tasks (taking out the garbage, cleaning up the family room, meals on the weekends etc.)
- The parties agree the Wife will call a realtor to get an estimate of the house's value and the Husband will call a financial advisor to help determine the best way to divide the other assets.

Frequently, when agreements such as these are made, they don't need immediate legal documentation. At some point, some decisions, like the last one above, may need legal documents to protect each of their interests if they are truly committing to a legal position. Sometimes, legal documents need to be provided before a decision can be made, like tax returns.

Some spouses think hiding information is beneficial. That is BS. Most divorce lawyers will tell you that is one of the most foolish things someone who is getting divorced can do. In addition to the fact that a Judge may considered it a fraud on the court, the hidden asset could be taken away from the spouse who attempted to hide it and given to the spouse from whom it was hid. The assets and liabilities are what they are. Trying to outmaneuver the system usually fails. It is expensive to try to get away from reality...that is No BS.

To get agreements on potentially disputed assets, do the following:

1. **Agree to use an outside source for determining value of assets.** If one appraisal is unsatisfactory, suggest another.

2. **Speak with your accountant to about the tax consequences of selecting or not selecting each asset.**

3. **Prepare two lists dividing property, one you prefer and one you can live with.**

4. **Suggest that an asset that the two of you cannot agree on be given to the children instead of one spouse.**

5. **Trade assets.** All assets do not have to be split in

half. You can trade one asset for another. This is frequently done when the equity for a house is traded for the equity in a retirement account. Both parties retain the same net worth, just in different assets. This is often done with stock, cash, pensions, IRAs, place settings of china, etc.

6. **Determine which assets are income producers or have the highest likelihood of producing income and assign those to the lower earner.** This is often done with rental property.

7. **Consider separating assets out of the assets to be divided.** This is often done for children's college accounts. Those accounts can be considered the children's and not be divided between the parties.

8. **Discuss whether it is possible to share an item.** This is a typical resolution for a family vacation home or time share.

9. **Use joint funds to buy one spouse a duplicate of a marital asset which will retained by the other spouse.** Marital funds are often used to purchase children's beds for the new house of a spouse.

A successful resolution of these difficult issues is the result of hard work, precise timing, emotional and financial sensitivity and flexibility on the part of both parties and the professionals they employ. *A secret*…Negotiate in good faith, speak the truth in the moment but know that things change, people change and the divorce isn't over until it's over.

Chapter Five:
Financial Impact of Divorce on Families

Reviewing Financial Information

One or both parties will suffer economically from a divorce. That is No BS. Sometimes men earn more than women. Sometimes women earn more than men. Sometimes a spouse has not been in the work force for years. Statistically, men usually earn more that women and women have been out of the workforce at some point during the marriage. As a result, financial analysts frequently report that men often retain, on a per capita basis, considerably more income and assets than women after a divorce. They point to data, sometimes considered evidence, that a woman is almost always in worse financial shape than a man as a result of a divorce. They also report that men are often better able to recoup financially and much faster than women. Although is sounds sexist, it is No BS. The statistical reality is that a man's ability to become financially stable within a few years after a divorce is much greater and much quicker than woman's.

In a typical divorce, the marital assets and liabilities are the starting point in dividing assets equally or relatively equally. From there, the post divorce financial needs of the spouses and financial support of the children are taken into consideration when assessing whether an agreement is "fair." Statistically, children are more frequently placed with and end up in the Mother's residential care. The Mother's financial share of the marital estate is used to support her and the children. The Father's financial share of the marital estate, reduced by amounts from his income or estate to provide for the children and sometimes the former spouse, is typically used to support him. Per capita, that is, per person, the man's estate and his net worth is often greater than the woman's, even if he is giving her a generous settlement just because he is supporting one person and she is supporting herself and others.

To be able to adequately plan for current and future financial needs, spouses have to become familiar with and understand the financial state of the marriage. Preparing a Financial Information Worksheet, which includes both income and expense information, will help to identify what the true financial picture of the marriage looks like. When someone is contemplating a divorce, it is often necessary to find, itemize, and inventory the existing assets and liabilities. Most lawyers will want prepared income and expense statements from clients so that the lawyer can properly advise the client on different financial settlement options. Usually there are standardized forms which are used to gather that information. These forms are often the starting point for determining what exists, who has what, who needs what and who gets what. Every line item on these forms helps the client decide what needs to be decided, what needs to be reviewed, what adjustments should be made and what options can be considered. The forms begin to provide the basis of what the current and future needs of the family will be as well as what is realistically possible for the family given the financial health of the marriage. They are also helpful when spouses are looking at or trying to find creative ways to decrease expenses and/or increase income.

It is often a good idea to get some insight from a financial planner or an accountant. For some items, there are legal formulas that are used to determine amounts, such as the appropriate amount of child support and spousal support. The IRS does not provide a tax deduction for the payment of child support. Child support is not deductible by the payer. The recipient does not have to pay income taxes on child support. The IRS does provide a tax deduction for the payment of spousal support. Spousal support is deductible by the payer and the recipient pays income taxes on the amount they receive. The IRS also allows a tax deduction for certain agreements that provide for family support. Family support is deductible to the payer and taxable to the payee. Agreements about financial support take into consideration both spouses financial needs. A financial planner or divorce attorney generally calculates the amounts for the client. The amounts calculated by the professionals are usually the amounts the parties should use when negotiating how the financial needs of the family will be met once the divorce has been finalized.

Sometimes it is helpful to use a step-by-step process to divide marital property and debts.

Here's an example of a step-by-step approach:

1. **Agree that all agreements regarding the division of property, debts and all other issues are tentative until final decisions are made.** No agreement is really final until it is in writing, both spouses agree and have signed it, a Judge has signed it and entered it as a court order.

2. **Remember you and your spouse can change your minds about any property and debt divisions up until the agreement is legally binding.** Since each of you has the right to change your minds on all issues, don't make any major financial moves, like buying a home, until you know the agreement will be honored.

3. **Prepare a complete financial disclosure statement.** It could be a balance sheet, it could be a court form and it could be the one suggested in the No BS Divorce Workbook. List all assets. List all debts. Determine which assets and debts you consider joint and which you consider belonging to one of the spouses. Identify which of you will responsible for which joint debts and which of you will take individual responsibility for which separate debts.

4. **Assess a value, if known or if possible, to all assets.** Agree on a procedure to obtain the value for the items when the value is unknown. There are

many ways to do that. Some people make up a value based on their sense of fairness. Others have an independent third party appraise property. If property is going to be appraised, decide whether the appraisal will be the final word on the asset's value or if a second opinion might be required. Others decide that each party will solicit their own outside source for an opinion regarding the value of an asset. If each spouse is going to get their own opinion, decide what to do if the values are far apart, decide how to resolve the difference, perhaps average the results. There is no one correct way to establish values for property. Establishing a value that both parties think is fair is the hard part. That is No BS.

5. **Determine whether you will ignore the monetary value of any items.** For example, people often consider certain items as being equal, such as personal property (linens, silverware, pots, pans, lamps, etc.). Ignoring monetary value is often appropriate for household furniture and furnishing. Judges will divide each individual item when called upon to do so, but it is an expensive proposition. People can often take what they want and understand that it is not possible to have an entirely equal, dollar-for-dollar distribution.

BALANCE SHEET: PRE -DIVORCE

ASSETS/LIABILITIES	TOTAL
Retirement accounts	$100,000
House (net)	$200,000
Car 1	$25,000
Car 2	$10,000
Credit Card 1	($5,000)
Credit Card 2	($2,000)
TOTAL	$328,000
Non-marital	$50,000
NET ASSETS	$378,000

6. **Create different ways about how you might to distribute all the assets and debts.** Will you each get an equal share of each asset? Will one party get more than half? Will you value all assets and divide them so that each of you has the same net worth but different assets? Are there assets you wish to retain that you may have to "trade" other assets for? Good legal advice regarding asset and debt division can eliminate confusing negotiations and hard feelings after the divorce.

7. **Sometimes parties bring property and debts into the marriage.** This is often referred to as "non-marital" property. What a spouse brought to a marriage is usually theirs to keep, but do not assume that this is always the case. Make sure you have good legal advice on this issue. True non-marital prop-

erty retains its non-marital status. For example, if the Husband brought his grandmother's rocking chair into the marriage, it is his to take when he leaves the marriage. However, having non-marital property may affect the final distribution of marital assets. Having significant non-marital assets may mean that the marital assets are divided more favorably to your spouse. This is a great question to ask the lawyer with whom you are consulting and considering retaining.

A tentative property and debt split may look like this:

BALANCE SHEET: POST-DIVORCE

ASSETS/LIABILITIES	TOTAL	SPOUSE A	SPOUSE B
Retirement accounts	$100,000	$50,000	$50,000
House (net)	$200,000	$100,000	$100,000
Car 1	$25,000	$25,000	
Car 2	$10,000		$10,000
Credit Card 1	($5,000)	($3,500)	($1,500)
Credit Card 2	($2,000)		($2,000)
TOTAL*	$328,000	$171,500	$156,500
Non-marital	$50,000		$50,000
NET ASSETS*	$378,000	$171,500	$206,500

*Note: Determine if allocation should be adjusted for fairness.

Chapter Six:
The Process....It's Going to Cost You

But Behind the Scenes — What Really Happens?

People often say that they just don't understand what happens in a divorce. They don't understand why seemingly sane and loving people turn into insane, spiteful people. Unless you've actually been divorced and have gone through it, you may only know about it through family or friends, the tabloids (Brittany and Kevin, Ivana and Donald, Alec and Kim), the movies ("War of the Roses," "The Story of Us," "The Betty Broderick Story," "Parent Trap") or sitcoms ("The New Adventures of Old Christine," "Reba").

What happens in the legal process to get a divorce is really simple and straightforward. One person asks the court for the divorce, both parties agree on the division of assets and liabilities and the schedule of time children spend between the two homes and the Judge approves the agreement. It is done. It is that simple.

But, spouses usually complicate the process. They involve and well over-involve lawyers and Judges. In the legal process, everyone, the parties, the attorneys and the Judge are bound by and required to follow a set of rules and laws which are set up to get a dispute ready for a trial. However, since 97% of cases never go to trial before a Judge, the legal process may be more than what is needed to come up with settlement terms. Of course there are those issues and clients who will go to trial. The remaining three percent. If you know you are in the 97% of all divorce cases and you know you won't have a trial, then it makes sense to spend as little time and money on the legal process as you possibly can. That does require however open-mindedness to possible settlement terms, especially those proposed by your spouse, willingness to work with your spouse to get the matter concluded and honesty about which options you can live with and which ones you cannot. Two spouses can be as creative as they want to be.

Here is a simple example. When two parents are trying to decide how many extra-curricular activities their two children should be involved in at the same time, they investigate volleyball, soccer, basketball, football, church groups, ballet, hip hop, tennis and bowling. Lots of things they like. Their next door neighbor may investigate piano lessons and ballet. Both families are planning for and providing the experiences they want their children to have. There is no right, wrong, good or bad. Both families are making good, although different decisions. The same is true for spouses who are negotiating settlement terms. Settlements and settlement terms will be different for most families, but they all work. This is true no matter whether the parties are developing a parenting plan or a division of assets and liabilities.

As stated in Chapter Two, researching your lawyer, your lawyer's reputation in the social and legal communities, your lawyer's weekly schedule and their philosophy on how to handle divorce matters gives you useful information that you will need to select an attorney. Doing your homework and interviewing a few lawyers will ensure that you are more likely to select the lawyer who best suits your personality, your financial situation and your settlement style.

Most lawyers who practice exclusively in family and matrimonial law are members of a rather small legal group, known in the legal community and to each other. They are likely known by your friends, your hairdresser or bartender. Clients like to talk and get feedback about divorce lawyers. Because it is a tight knit group of professionals, clients can misinterpret our relationships, especially when it's the relationship between their lawyer and their spouse's lawyer. It may be surprising to learn that as a legal community, lawyers know each other, generally like each other and often socialize together.

In our business, countless clients come and go but we will see each other every day, year after year. We will be on both the winning and losing side of lots of cases. Don't worry that your lawyers are working well together and not screaming at each other to get this matter done for your family. Don't worry that in court they are calm and rational and not interrupting your spouse's lawyer when that lawyer makes a statement that makes your teeth hurt. The courtroom is a professional setting. In that setting you want a professional representing you, not a ranting fool. The ranting fool often creates more problems for the client than the client has trying to negotiate with their spouse.

The family law business is a business that does not usually have repeat customers. We family law lawyers have to continually generate new business to keep our business thriving. The family law business is the business we lawyers selected to provide for our financial needs and that of our families. It is our job. We strive to treat both our businesses and our clients in a professional, businesslike manner.

No matter how much divorce clients appreciate their divorce lawyers, chances are quite good that they will not be comfortable referring a friend or family member to their divorce lawyer's office. Even although divorce lawyers are bound by attorney/client privilege, sometimes clients worry that we lawyers will discuss their matter with our friends, their friends and even their family. Ethically, we cannot discuss your case with anyone. The only information which is not confidential is that information which the client put in the public record, discussed with friends or put on the internet. And if we were going to talk about our cases, our current cases and clients are much more interesting to us than talking about or rehashing old clients and old cases.

Unless a divorce case involves unusual facts or circumstances or may be establishing new law, many of our cases are similar in facts and results. Like anyone that has a job, whether they like it or they don't, the last thing lawyers want to do is go home or go out with friends and start talking about our work.

Here's our schedule in a typical week. Most family law attorneys start their day early. We arrive at our offices early, often before we go to court. We are usually in court four mornings a week. Court sessions generally begins at 8, 8:30 or 9 a.m. Depending upon the number of cases we have that morning or the number that the court has on its schedule, we could be in court for an hour or until noon. On those days that we have a case that goes to trial, we often are in court the entire day until the court room closes. Courtrooms close between 4:30 and 5 on most days but can go into the evening. In family law cases, it happens on occasion that a matter may go into the night but generally not. Unlike criminal cases with juries, divorce cases tend to end before dinner.

When we have completed our court business, usually around 11 a.m. or noon, we head back to the office. We talk with our secretaries, help the secretary handle any matters they can handle and then we prepare for our afternoon. Our afternoons and evenings are frequently dedicated to client appointments and meetings. When we meet with our clients, we usually do not take phone calls or let our staff interrupt us for any reason. We want to dedicate that meeting time to that client or prospective client who is in our office or who has scheduled a phone appointment.

Most of us try to retrieve client calls and voice mail messages and answer calls while we are out of the office. Most lawyers try to call their office and return client calls as soon as they have a break in their morning at court. We cannot predict when that break will be and even if we could, we don't carry every client's file or phone number with us. As technologically savvy as many of us are and as wonderful as Blackberrys and I-Phones can be, many of us don't have our clients' phone numbers stored in our phones. We don't have the numbers we need to return calls when we are away from the office. In addition to trying to return client calls when we get a minute at the courthouse or when we are court waiting for another case to be called, we try to return calls when we are driving back to the office and when we are running errands.

Once we get back to our office, there is little time for us to return calls. Often we have our staff handle the calls that do not require our legal expertise. It is easier for us to return calls to clients who leave phone numbers and specific questions. These types of calls are easier to return because we can leave a detailed message answering our client's questions. Being able to answer a client's question when we return their a call is easier for us and better for the client because we can leave a message and answer to their question, even if we do not actually speak with each other.

Attorney disciplinary commissions report that the number one client complaint is that lawyers don't return client calls. It is easy to see why that might happen. If your lawyer is not available when you telephone, it is good practice to leave a detailed message that includes your phone number and a good time to call you back. Telephone tag is a frequent occurrence, it will happen. By giving your lawyer the opportunity to respond to your question, you will avoid unnecessary frustration for yourself and help your lawyer do a better job for you.

In every courthouse, there is a well established procedure for how divorce cases are handled. When you understand the procedural timeline, you will have an idea of just how long the divorce process might be and what the costs involved might be. The timeline shown in Chapter Four is similar to the timeline in most courtrooms around the country.

This can be surprising news to a spouse considering a divorce. People who believe that their divorce will be resolved in a short time are often appalled when they learn that the legal procedure may take as long as 18 months or longer. They often don't know that they can be divorced as soon as they and their spouse agree on settlement terms about the assets, liabilities and children. When you know the legal system's timeline, you can plan your schedule accordingly. You will know whether or not your case will be completed before or after the Christmas holiday. You will plan that holiday in a good way for children if you know whether or not everyone will be together or if they will be with you or if they will be with your spouse. You will know whether or not you will be divorced before or after the house sells. You will make better long-term decisions while you are living in the limbo of getting separated or divorced.

The legal timeline affects the cost of a divorce. The specific costs based on a traditional divorce and a No BS Divorce are explained in Chapter Two.

Don't hesitate to ask your lawyer about the strengths and weaknesses of a particular legal strategy. Although the divorce process is often unpredictable, lawyers who regularly practice family law can estimate your timeline based on the accuracy of the information you provide regarding your spouse's level of cooperation, your motivation and the information he or she has about your spouse's lawyer and your Judge. Have your lawyer advise you about how the timeline would be if you and your spouse worked things out and the legal process was relatively simple. Have him or her also advise you about how the timeline would be if you agreed about most, but not all issues. Have him or her outline the timeline if the matter went to trial. Your divorce attorney can pretty accurately estimate the timeline for you, including the time needed to verify financial matters and child-related issues. Your lawyer will also be able to clearly explain costs so that you can make informed decisions and get closer to resolution.

Decisions regarding any particular proposal for settlement of financial aspects will have substantial effects on you and your future. You will live with the consequences, good and bad of those decisions. You are responsible for the financial, emotional, physical and spiritual decisions of your case. You should make all the substantive decisions. Your lawyer is an expert in the procedural workings of the court system. Because divorce lawyers are familiar with the workings of the court system, they are primarily responsible for procedural decisions that affect your case and will make all the procedural decisions.

Before you finalize any substantive decision, you will have the opportunity to discuss any and all settlement proposals with your lawyer, your family and your friends. As stated in Chapter Two, once you begin this divorce journey, well-intended friends and strangers will give you good and bad advice. They will try to spare you the financial ruin they or, worse, someone they know experienced. Each divorce case is unique and each person lives with the results of the decisions they make, good or bad, motivated by a good or bad purpose. You may want to seek out only those trusted friends who will give you good advice that truly fits your needs.

Your lawyer will give you advice based on a number of possible outcomes. The outcomes can be effected by how well you and your spouse work together on the disputed issues, whether the matter settles due to your efforts or the efforts of each of your attorneys or a combination of both and whether the matter is submitted to the court for a decision because the case going to trial

Lawyers endeavor to keep you regularly informed of the progress of your case. When you think you need more information more frequently, just ask.

Here's *a secret*. My ideal client is one who helps me do a good job for them. It is someone I like and someone who likes me. My ideal client pays my bill on time. They tell me what they can do and they do it. They tell me what they can't do before I find out they can't do something. They plan and schedule time to talk to me or meet with me when they need to. They ask me the questions that they have. They provide me with the information I need when I request it in the way I can get to it quickly. (For example, it takes longer for me to review three years of bank statements that are still in the original envelops than it takes to review the statements that are open and in chronological order.) They assess the strengths and weaknesses of their spouse correctly. When the divorce is over, their spouse refers their best friend to me to handle their divorce.

Chapter Seven:
The Options...
So It Doesn't Cost You...
Pick Your Settlement Path

Forms of Dispute Resolution: Litigation, Mediation

Many people think the only way to get a divorce is to go through the trauma of litigation. Litigation, sometimes called adjudication, is the most formal dispute resolution process and almost always the most expensive process to get a divorce. That is No BS. Litigation begins when a spouse files a complaint, which in a divorce case is a petition for divorce, and requests that the court grant the divorce. This is a lawsuit between spouses. Once the petition has been filed and the case started, it can only end with a settlement about assets, liabilities and children in a trial where witnesses are called to testify before a Judge or a dismissal of the case.

Litigation takes place in a courtroom with rules of evidence and formal courtroom procedures, although many pieces of litigation, such as depositions, occur outside of the courtroom. Testimony is presented by witnesses to develop the facts of the case. The lawyers research the relevant law and the applicability of the law to the facts. The Judge takes all of the pieces and determines the outcome after the trial. Lawyers, Judges, litigants and witnesses are the central figures in this process. If a matter goes to trial, the client has two options: win or lose.

There are good reasons for litigation of disputes, although not necessarily for divorce disputes. Litigation makes law for society and the community as a whole while it is resolving an individual dispute. In litigation, Judges prefer the participation by the parties but if someone fails to participate the process does not stop. When a person decides that they are not going to participate in the litigation process, it almost always guarantees their opponent, their spouse, will win and be awarded what they asked for in the initial petition, even if the allegations in the petition cannot be proven. Failure to participate may result in losing the chance to defend oneself, losing the chance to secure one's property or even losing the case. Once a lawsuit has been filed, especially a divorce case, the spouse being sued is best served by participating in the legal process.

Here are some litigation terms you should know:

1. **Complaint Petition**—The complaint is the document in a divorce called the petition, which states the legal theory the complaining party (the Petitioner) relies upon, the facts they believe to be true and the relief they are asking the court to provide. In a divorce case, the correct designation is Petition.

2. **Service / Service of Process**—A person is served with the complaint, the Petition for Dissolution of Marriage document and a summons from the court, by either the sheriff or special process server.

The Sheriff has served someone when he or she personally hands the document to the spouse or someone eighteen years and older who lives with them. Service gives the court the jurisdiction, the ability, to make decisions for the parties when the parties have not done so.

3. **Petitioner/Plaintiff**—The Petitioner is the person in the divorce case who is initiating the legal process. They are the one who has petitioned, requested, the Court to grant them a divorce. Although the terms Petitioner and plaintiff are sometimes used interchangeably, in a divorce case, the correct designation is Petitioner.

4. **Respondent/Defendant**—The Respondent is the person in the divorce case who is to respond to the legal process. They are the one who has not petitioned, requested or asked the Court to grant them a divorce. Although the terms Respondent and defendant are sometimes used interchangeably, in a divorce case, the correct designation is Respondent.

5. **Counter Petition**—The Counter Petition is the document which a Respondent spouse who wants a divorce may file. It states the legal theory the responding party (the Respondent) relies upon, the facts they believe to be true and the relief they are

asking the Court to provide. In a divorce case, one reason to file a counter petition is that if the spouse who files a petition decides to withdraw their petition, the Counter Petitioner can still proceed with a divorce, even although the original Petitioner may no longer want one.

6. **Four Way Conference** —The Four Way Conference is an attempt to settle the case between the lawyers and the parties. Four people, the Husband, the Wife, the Husband's attorney and the Wife's attorney meet to see if settlement is possible. It is also the time the lawyers use to size up their case. It is the lawyer's opportunity to see if the opposing spouse will be a good witness, if the client has accurately portrayed their spouse, what the other spouse's lawyer thinks are the strengths and weaknesses of both versions of the case.

7. **Pretrial Conferences** —The pretrial conference is another attempt to resolve the matter, settle the case, prior to trial. Unlike the Four Way Conference where the parties and their lawyers participate, in a Pretrial cConference usually only the Judge and the lawyers participate. They discuss, usually for a specified amount of time, the respective positions of each client, the strengths and weaknesses of the evidence and the likelihood of success for each party on each issue. In a pretrial, the Judge usually

gives suggestions for ways in which the case may be settled. He or she also gives insight into how he or she might rule on a particular dispute based upon the information the lawyers present to him. In a Pretrial Conference, the lawyers are told what the Judge will do if the parties decide to take the matter to trial. The Judge makes those recommendations based upon an assumption that the evidence that will be proved in a trial will be substantially the same evidence that the lawyers represented to the Judge during the Pretrial Conference.

8. **Trial** —The Trial is the ultimate adversarial process and it is the final word on any disputes between spouses. During the Trial, the Judge will determine the outcomes regarding the parenting plan for the children, the division of assets and the responsibilities for liabilities. The Judge is in charge of and conducts the Trial. He or she will rule on the evidence and the questions of law. In a divorce trial, the Petitioner has the burden of providing evidence which establishes that the court should grant the divorce and decide the matter in the way in which the Petitioner wants. The Respondent can merely respond or offer explanations contrary to the Petitioner's position.

9. **Post Trial** —Sometimes cases are really not done when the trial is over and divorces are not final.

There is an appeal process that can be requested if a spouse thinks the Judge was unfair. To have an appeal or new trial, something had to be wrong with the fairness or administration of the original trial.

Litigation can be supplemented with other forms of dispute resolution. In family law, mediation is a common practice to resolve disputes, especially custody disputes. Mediation is an informal, non-adversarial process in which a third party acts as a facilitator. That third party, the mediator, is a neutral facilitator. Their job is to help the parties resolve the disputes that are preventing them from reaching a final settlement. Most family disputes can be mediated. Frequently spouses go to mediation to work out parenting time schedules, divide assets and determine of how bills will be paid.

Unlike a Judge, the mediator is selected by agreement of the parties or by the lawyers. Often the divorce lawyers have a good sense of which mediator is a good match for the client and their spouse. In many jurisdictions, when parenting issues like custody and visitation are not resolved by the parties, mediators are appointed by Judges. Mediators do not have the power to impose a solution on the parties but they frequently come up with creative options to get the matter settled.

Mediation is sometimes defined as a process in which a neutral third person, the mediator, acts to encourage and assist the resolution of a dispute between two or more parties. Its primary objective is to help the disputing parties reach mutually acceptable agreements on all or many of the issues in dispute. The key distinguishing feature of mediation is that the mediator is not the decision-maker. Decision-making authority rests with the parties, not the mediator.

One of the mediator's goal is to help the parties reach agreements that are acceptable to each of them, not the agreement the mediator thinks is best. Another goal in mediation is to forecast where conflict will arise in the future. The emphasis in mediation is on spouses working together toward a solution that benefits both of them. The theory is that the spouses create a win-win solution, rather than a solution which pits one party against another and where one party wins and one party loses.

One of the mediator's functions is to assist the parties in identifying issues, encouraging joint problem-solving and exploring settlement alternatives.

Mediation is one of the oldest forms of dispute resolution. It can be quick, private, relatively inexpensive, reasonably priced and informal. Mediation can preserve relationships between the parties. It can empower spouses to arrive at their own, custom-tailored solutions. In mediation, like most settlement discussions, parties are not limited to predictable legal outcomes, remedies or the lawyers and Judge's ideas. In mediation, parties often reach agreements that a Judge might not be able to order. For example, in most states, Judges cannot require parents to live within a certain mile radius of each other. In mediation, parents frequently enter into those agreements. They do so because they want their spouse to stay within a certain mile range of them, they want their children to be in a certain school district and they want their children to be treated at a certain hospital. Mediation is most effective when both parties have the ability and desire to negotiate in their own best interests.

The mediator is in charge of and controls the process. He or she also assists the spouses to determine which issues need the expertise of an outside consultant. People other than the spouses may participate in mediation although that is at the discretion of the mediator. A mediator may terminate a mediation session or terminate all future mediation session when he or she believes that continuing the process would harm one or more of the parties or the children. The mediator can also terminate mediation when he or she believes that the ability or willingness of any spouse to participate meaningfully is so lacking that a reasonable agreement is unlikely.

When terminating the mediation session, mediators are not required to provide an explanation for the termination. They may elect to state a reason, but do not have to. The parties can terminate mediation at any time unless there is a court order requiring them to participate in mediation.

Mediation can be successful when the parties are willing to participate in the mediation process, are familiar with the financial state of the marriage, are in agreement about what is in the children's best interest and have the ability to negotiate in their own best interests.

Litigation focuses on findings of fact about events that occurred in the past. Mediation focuses on the future and the potential for future disputes and the mediator helps the spouses agree to future conduct that will be required to resolve their dispute.

In my experience, people who mediate their divorce case before it is finalized often are better able to problem solve when issues arise in the future. They also tend to see the cost benefit of using mediation when conflicts arise years after the divorce is finalized. There is huge financial and emotional savings to be had when people don't have to go back to court.

Chapter Eight:
Gathering Information...
Show Me the Money

Any time a partner is considering a divorce, they will need all types of information. Their lawyers will ask them to provide different things and each of the spouses will be required to produce copies of all of it. Such information and documents include copies of tax returns, real estate documents including closing statements, bank statements, credit card statements, business records and a variety of other documents.

It doesn't matter how far along in the process the spouses are or at what stage the lawyer is retained, financial information will needed to be verified before settlement agreements can be finalized. Usually when a spouse consults with a lawyer they provide preliminary, unverified, information. Once they select and retain a lawyer, that lawyer will usually have the client fill out a detailed information and fact sheet. They will request very specific financial information which they will need in order to adequately advise the client of their legal position and prepare the settlement options.

The best way to gather and collect financial and really all subjective information is to ask your spouse to work with you, specify what is needed and divide up the work. This is not easy for either spouse to do and it is particularly difficult because it usually comes at a time when the marriage has broken down and communication between the spouses is non-existent or very strained. It can be made more challenging because it is also the time when each spouse is suspicious and is questioning every request the other partner makes.

So how do you get the information? Go through the files the family has maintained throughout the marriage. Make a list of the missing documents and ask your spouse to provide them. If they don't have them or refuse to provide them, try to get them from the original source, for example the bank. But just because a spouse doesn't voluntarily provide the information you request, they will be required to produce it. Your lawyer can issue a subpoena or request to produce that requires your spouse to provide documents. It just will be more costly.

Chapter Four suggests some ways of getting information directly from your spouse.

The following are topics which need to be discussed between the two spouses when one or both of them is contemplating a separation or divorce.

1. **How and when will we separate or divorce?**

2. **What will we do about the children?** When will they be with Mom, when will they be with Dad? How long can a parent take a child for a vacation, a vacation each parent and the child will enjoy?

3. **Who will be the residential parent for tax pur-**

poses, college applications and such?

4. **Where will each of us live? In this state or in another state?**

5. **What will the parenting time schedule look like?** Will the schedule be the same during the school year, the summer, school breaks, holidays and days off from school? Can we telephone and email the kids when they are with the other parent?

6. **What will we do about the children's financial issues?** Who will pay child support? What expenses are covered and what is not by child support? What expenses will be shared? Will children's extracurricular activities, child care, health insurance, dental and vision insurance, out of pocket medical expenses, life insurance and automobile insurance be shared? Who gets the tax deduction for the children? How will the children's college expenses be paid?

7. **Who gets what marital property,** including the house, the business, cars, furniture, bank accounts, stocks, bonds and notes, retirement, pension, profit-sharing and annuities and savings accounts?

8. **Who gets what debt,** including the mortgage, the

student loans and the credit card debt?

9. **How will we go about the divorce process?** How will we use lawyers, mediators, therapists and other professionals? Who will file? When will we be done?

Chapter Nine:
The Real Issues...It's Always About the Money

Child Support, Spousal Support, the Family Residence, the Family Business, The Retirement Accounts and more...

Most states have guidelines about how to divide the financial matters of a marriage. The most common financial issues are child support, spousal support, the family residence, the family business and the retirement accounts. This is a quick commentary on each of the areas, but be sure to check with your lawyer before finalizing any financial matters.

Child support—Most states have laws or at least guidelines and suggestions about how child support will be paid, who will pay and how much will be paid. Child support is typically paid for children who are 18 and under and who have not yet graduated from high school. It is also paid for high school students who are 19.

Couples can determine their own child support arrangements as long as the arrangement meets the legal requirements. Sometimes Judges have concerns about the financial agreements made between parents which are different from the guidelines set down in the laws. They worry that one spouse has coerced the other spouse into accepting less than what the legal requirements are. The legal requirements are designed to protect the financial well-being of the children, not the parents. Sometimes parents will try to get custody of the children to avoid paying child support. Judge's are very in tune to those tactics but that's a topic for another day.

Child support and the amount of support that a parent will have to pay for the support of the children can be determined based on the children's needs and circumstances. The guidelines are a piece of information to be considered but they are not the only factors to consider when setting an amount to be paid.

Parents should be realistic when they consider and calculate how much the children's expenses are. Some parents over estimate them, other parents underestimate them. Some parents don't care, they just don't want to ever have to talk about money with their former spouse ever again. Child and child related expenses include costs for such things as medical insurance premiums, out-of-pocket medical expenses, day care expenses, extracurricular expenses for activities and sports, teacher gifts and birthday parties. They may include musical instruments or music lessons.

When parents are able to agree on the amount of regularly paid support for the children and the payment of any additional support amounts the child will require, they will keep themselves out of the courthouse. If parents are able to decide when the child support will increase or decrease, they will minimize or entirely eliminate the cost to go back to court in the future and spend money to get money. Cases involving the recalculation or collection of child support often end up costing more money than the parent can recover or collect. When one or both parties are looking at and assessing how best to keep the money in the family, they can create opportunities for keeping the money between them. Whether the parent receiving child support gets it or the parent paying child support keeps it, the children will invariably benefit.

When people have unresolved conflicts between them or are not able to settle disputes, it is not uncommon for one of them to pay his or her lawyer $2,500 or more to file a petition with the court requesting a $1,000 increase or decrease of child support. They are willing to pay a lawyer two and a half times more than what they owe or might owe their former spouse. Parents sometimes want to pay lawyers to handle child support cases which require them to pay us thousands of dollars to collect hundreds. Who benefits? Our children. Too often, the family would be better served financially and emotionally if one or both of them would consider the cost benefits of pursuing these types of matters...and that is No BS.

To determine what the financial needs of a family will be after the divorce is concluded, a Judge will often take into consideration the following: the financial resources and needs of each individual, the standard of living the family would have enjoyed had the marriage not been dissolved, the physical and emotional conditions of the individuals, any special needs of the children and what the Judge believes is reasonable in the community.

Most states require support to be stated in the court order as a dollar amount rather than a percentage amount. In some cases, it may be in both the children's and the parents' best interests to decide whether an annual increase or decrease in child support is appropriate and, if so, when will it be effective. Some couples decide that the Judge should calculate the adjustments every three years. Some couples decide that it is just easier to hire a lawyer and let the legal system handle it. No matter what the procedure is to adjust support in the future, it is easier for both parents to budget their resources if they know the exact dollar amount to be paid, the frequency it is to be paid and when it will be increased or decreased.

Spousal support —Parties decide the amount of spousal support (sometimes called maintenance or alimony) as they divide up their assets. Spousal support is awarded to a spouse for a variety of reasons. Those reasons vary in every state. In most states, there are some factors which automatically trigger a discussion of spousal support. Those factors include how long the parties were married, how old they are, whether or not they worked outside the home during the marriage. Settlement agreements can provide for spousal support payments that are limited in time as well as spousal support payments that increase or decrease over time. They can also set conditions for when the spousal support will terminate.

There are many reasons why spousal support is a financial option for families. It is usually deductible on the payer's tax return and is taxable to the payee. Typically, the payer is in a higher tax bracket and the payee is in a lower tax bracket, so the deduction is a benefit for the payer and because the tax rate is relatively low for the payee, the family pays less income taxes. Typical agreements require spousal support to terminate on a set date or after a certain number of payments have been made. It can also terminate when the payee spouse remarries or when one of the parties dies. It is a good idea to talk with your tax advisor or divorce attorney to decide whether spousal support will save the family some money and if it is appropriate given your facts.

Better yet...unallocated family support—Sometimes the deal of the day, at least as it relates to paying less taxes to Uncle Sam, is to combine both the child support obligation with the spousal support obligation as "unallocated family support." In cases where unallocated family support is appropriate, it allows the payer to deduct all payments made to the payee on his or her income tax return. The payee pays taxes on all payments received. The trick is to make sure that the payee spouse is not being paid less than they would have received if child support and maintenance were paid separately. If it turns out that the payee spouse would get less than what they would otherwise be entitled to, it can be easily remedied. The simplest way is to have the accountant or divorce attorney calculate the amount of taxes the payee would have to pay on the amount received. Then increase the total support amount to be paid by the payer by the amount of the payee's tax liability. This is frequently, but not always, a good solution for families and it keeps more money in the family and less being paid for taxes. Have the attorney or the accountant prepare the language for unallocated family support agreements. If not carefully drafted, the wrong termination event could create a situation where the IRS disallows the deductions. This is the kind of question you want to pay your lawyer to answer. That is No BS.

The family residence—Decisions about keeping or selling the family residence evoke a lot of discussion and frequently conflict. For a variety of reasons, one spouse may wish to retain the family residence. One spouse may want to sell it. Often, the spouse with whom the children will reside wants to keep the residence whether or not it is financially feasible. A market analysis will establish a value range for the residence. Knowing what the value of the residence is may simplify or complicate the settlement negotiations. Knowing the value provides the information that a spouse needs to have in order to determine whether or not they can financially maintain the residence. If there is equity in the residence, they can determine if they qualify for a mortgage or if they have enough marital assets to exchange if they want to trade other assets to keep the residence. They also learn whether the residence should be sold.

The family business —When a family business is one of the assets to be divided, usually the spouse most intimately involved in the family business often views the business as an asset that would be worthless without his/her personal services. The spouse who is less involved in the business thinks it is worth millions. A business appraiser will appraise the value of the business. Where necessary, the appraiser will include the intangible factor of "good will." An independent appraiser will have some objectivity when assessing value. Selecting a reasonably priced business appraiser whose goal is to establish an objective value, not to prepare a case for litigation, is money well spent. It is not uncommon to learn that the value is not what either of the spouses thought it might be and it is either higher or lower than they had estimated.

In addition to providing an estimated value, a good appraiser will help resolve price conflicts. The less involved spouse often views the family business as a "gold mine" or a "cash cow," and the more involved spouse views it as having little to no value.

All of the foreseeable consequences of continued joint ownership, sale, division of and reallocation of the business should be considered.

When spouses litigate these issues, it is very costly. Sometimes, when they can't agree on a value, both spouses employ experts to give an opinion of value for the business. That duplication of expense can be avoided when two people select a neutral appraiser whose opinion they agree to use even if the appraiser supports one position over the other.

The family business, like the family residence, is an asset which is very likely to trigger emotions and conflict during the settlement negotiations. When one party has an emotional attachment to the business and the other has an emotional attachment to the family residence, the numbers can be worked out. This doesn't create a problem when two people are committed to getting the asset and property they want, rather than splitting all assets across the board.

The long-term goal is to prevent the possibility of subsequent remorse which creates future conflict and left unresolved drives people back to court.

The retirement accounts —Retirement accounts come in a variety of forms. They often are the largest asset in a marriage. They can be pensions, IRAs, SEPs or Keoghs. They can be defined contribution plans or defined benefit plans. Some retirement plans have an "actuarial" value which differs from the value stated on the annual statement provided by the pension administrator. It is a wise to have an independent appraisal or valuation of all the retirement accounts before deciding to trade them for interest in other properties, like the equity in a home. The division of retirement plans can be tricky and risky if not done properly. If the proper court orders are not entered, it is possible for the person who is the named account holder to make withdrawals from the account. Those withdrawals could reduce the benefit to the other spouse. This is an issue where the money you pay for your lawyer's expertise can save you thousands of dollars and ensure that your agreed portion of those accounts is protected and available to you when your retirement time comes.

And more —Of course, there are many other financial matters. Assets like bank accounts, personal property, cars, art work, family photos and videos are usually not to difficult to divide. Liabilities like credit card debt, car loans or student loans are a bit more challenging. All of these, assets and liabilities, get allocated and distributed between the parties as part of the final settlement agreement. Creating a balance sheet is a good way to ensure that everything is provided for and allocated in the manner that you believe is fair. A sample is financial statement is found in the *No BS Divorce Workbook*.

Chapter Ten:
The Professionals...
Costs You Should Consider

Working with Outside Experts

When the spouses who are considering a divorce or have taken action toward getting the divorce, have a goal to keep the money in the family, making the best decisions about when and how to bring in outside professionals is essential. One or more outside professionals may be needed. Generally these professionals include:

- **A family law attorney.** As a family law attorney, I can say without reservation that the most important investment people make in their divorce is their divorce lawyer. This is not the time to hire someone based on price. Hiring a lawyer who practices exclusively in the area of family law will help to ensure that the settlement agreements between the spouses will not leave out vital information or have vague, multiple meanings that could cause challenges or misunderstandings. They will make sure that all the terms that are supposed to be in the agreement are and the ones that are not supposed to be in the agreement are not.

- **A therapist or mental health professional.** Counseling during this stress-filled time helps both spouses and their children cope with the natural changes and transitions a divorce brings. Both skills to dealing with new challenges and skills to deal with the new conflicts often need to be learned. A mental health professional is a great resource to keep everyone mentally healthy and to provide guidance about the interactions of the various personality types.

- **An accountant.** Tax consequences, both favorable and detrimental, are best handled by a tax accountant who deals regularly with taxes and families in transition. An accountant can make recommendations about financial plans that keeps the money in the family and out of the tax coffers. He or she can give advice on the ramifications of child and spousal support plans as well as property divisions.

- **A real estate appraiser.** When residential or commercial property is involved, a real estate appraiser can estimate the value of the property.

- **A business appraiser.** When a family owned business or an interest in a professional practice is at stake, a business appraiser can provide an opinion about the value of the business.

- **An actuary.** An actuary values retirement accounts

for certain types of pension plans. They can provide an estimate of present value for retirement accounts.

- **A financial planner.** Similar to the accountant, a financial planner can make recommendations regarding the long- and short-term finances. They can suggest asset allocation plans which meet the needs of the family. They can also provide guidance for setting up and living within a budget. Most can assist in long-term financial planning.

- **A bankruptcy attorney.** Hopefully, this professional will only be needed only as a last resort. A bankruptcy attorney can provide information about what types of bankruptcy a spouse may be eligible for. They can counsel the spouse on the long-term positive and negative aspects of filing for bankruptcy. They are well versed in structuring agreements which a bankruptcy court will approve.

- **A realtor.** A realtor with knowledge of the geographic area of the property and the houses that are similar to the house in question can give an estimate of value when appraising a family residence or other real property.

Using one or more outside professionals usually provides the information parties need to make informed decisions. Moreover, these professionals can explain financial impacts, and pros and cons of taking certain positions and make recommendations based upon your specific hopes for the future. Use them as you need to so you can make the best decisions for you, decisions you can live with for a long time.

Chapter Eleven:
Getting an Agreement that Will Sustain the Test of Time

Writing an Agreement, Drafting a Marital Settlement Agreement, MSA Review Session

In most cases, there are two documents standing between being married and being divorced. Those two documents are the parenting agreement (PA) and the marital settlement agreement (MSA). The parenting agreement sets out when the children are with Mom and when they are with Dad and some agreements about how the children will be raised. For the most part, even the most obstinate people agree on some basic things about their children's medical care, religious upbringing and education. The settlement agreement sets out the agreements about how the assets will be divided and how the liabilities will be paid.

So why do so many divorces take 18 months, two years or sometimes longer to get done? In my experience, lengthy divorces, and by that I mean any divorce which takes longer than six months, occur because the parties do not think about their settlement or the terms and issues they need to consider until months after the case was filed. In my opinion, other than making the decision to get a divorce, being stuck in legal limbo is among the worst things any divorcing party has to endure.

One of the most common complaints divorce lawyers hear from their clients is: "You or you and I went to court. I took time off of work. It cost me $500 and I am not divorced." This is the reality for many people who are in the legal system trying to get divorced.

The first and most important thing people need to do when contemplating a divorce is communicate with their spouses. But when people are contemplating a divorce they do the thing they should not do, they stop communicating with their spouse. Communicating involves sending information in a manner in which it can be received and acted upon. Some people are verbal, they need to say it. Some are audio, they need to hear it. And some are visual, they need to see it in a written form.

If you are a talker but your spouse needs to see something in writing, you can talk all day long but you will not be communicating information to your spouse. He or she will not receive the information you are trying to transmit, if you transmit it in your communication style, verbally and not in their communication style, visual. Knowing your own communication style and that of your spouse, especially if they are different (because they usually are), helps ensure that the information you are trying to communicate is actually received by the intended recipient.

The second most important thing people should do when contemplating a divorce is get a preliminary agreement—a draft, a boilerplate or some written settlement agreement from their lawyer. It will not be complete and it will not have all the terms and conditions that may end up in the final agreement. It may have terms and conditions that don't apply to your situation. It doesn't matter because nothing is agreed until your lawyer approves it, you sign it, your spouse signs it and the Judge signs it. Once you get the initial document, mark it up with your ideas. Give it to your spouse and tell him or her to read it, mark it up and get it back to you within some specified time frame. If your spouse can review, mark up and give you documents back in three days, give them a week to do it. If they need two weeks to do it, give them three.

Follow up with them on the scheduled return date. If they haven't given you their changes, give them another copy of yours. Keep the document going back and forth between you. That exercise will do a few things. First, it will make the divorce real for both spouses. Second, it will keep both spouses focused on the terms and agreements that need to be discussed. Third, it will get you divorced sooner.

Once the terms of an agreement are reached, those terms must be reduced to writing. Since you have been working with a written agreement you are almost there. Be cautious, however. That agreement that you and your spouse have been working on is not a final agreement. In some jurisdictions, agreements between spouses are suspect and frequently not binding, even if they are signed. A rule of thumb is that an agreement is not enforceable until the document is approved by and signed by a Judge.

Here's *a secret.* Just as many real estate transactions have a standardized form contract, most divorce lawyers have standardized form parenting agreements and settlement agreements. For a variety of reasons, many lawyers don't provide these documents to their clients at the onset of the representation. But if the lawyer will give the client preliminary settlement documents, the documents give the client a starting point in communicating with his or her spouse. The documents identify very specifically what clients need to be talking to their spouses about. It helps control the discussions about assets, liabilities and children.

In other words, by knowing the specific terms that need to be discussed, both parties are less likely to go off on tangents about things that the legal system doesn't care about, such as whether one of you is dating or which one of you wants the divorce. It is a tremendous waste of time and emotional energy to continue to fight over things that do not have a purpose in the legal system.

The goal for getting a settlement is to reduce the number of items to be resolved by the Judge. When the number of disputed items is at a minimum, keeping the money in the family becomes possible. Here's why. The more issues that a divorce lawyer needs to present during trial the higher the costs, the more days of trial, the more days of missed work and the fewer days spent with the children. If a typical divorce trial takes five days, the conservative cost of two lawyers at $200 per hour per lawyer is $400 per hour for both lawyers. If we have eight hours per five days, that is 40 hours. For two lawyers that is 80 hours. So, $400 x 80 is $32,000 just for the actual days of trial. That $32,000 would pay tuition for one child for two years at the University of Illinois. That does not include the cost for the trial preparation time, the additional daily preparation time each new day of trial brings and the work that has to be done once the trial is completed.

Now, if you settle enough issues to have only two days of trial, your cost will drop significantly. Even if everything else is the same except for the number of days of trial (now at $400 x 16 hours x two lawyers equalling $12,800). The difference between a five-day trial and a two-day trial is $32,000 - $12,800 or approximately $20,000... more than a year of college for one child in the same university.

Before finalizing any matter or signing off any legal documents, even if you think all issues have been successfully resolved, it is a good idea to sleep on it. Take your time when reviewing any legal document that you are going to sign. These are important agreements that you will live with or in spite of for a long time. You, not your divorce lawyer, will reap the benefits or suffer the consequences of the terms and conditions of the agreements. It may seem obvious but let me just say, make sure you read the documents, understand the agreement and understand that you are bound by its terms.

Chapter Twelve:
The Future...Conflict Resolution and Closure

Difficult Endings, Resolution, Closure

In some cases, the clients may not have resolved all the issues relating to the marriage or the divorce. They may not be done with disputes even after they sign the final settlement papers. Some spouses continue to grieve the loss and the demise of their marriage years after the divorce. For others, the loss of friends, the loss of time with the children, the loss of the relationship of someone they used to love and the loss of their physical surroundings are voids that take years to fill.

Months, perhaps years later, some spouses feel and even claim that he/she made an agreement under duress or while in a daze or just because they wanted to get out of the marriage or just because they wanted to be nice. Because of these very real scenarios I think the importance of discussing any and all agreements and concerns about the future based upon the agreements with the lawyer prior to signing any legal documents cannot be overstated.

Most people don't plan or think about the timing of their divorce or plan when it will be concluded. Being able to decide when the divorce will be final helps with closure and gives both spouses a sense of control over the process. When both spouses take an active role and make informed decisions about what assets they want, what liabilities they will be responsible for, how they will parent the children and when they will be divorced, they make better decisions.

Here are some things to consider when picking the date to finalize the divorce and to be divorced:

- **Income Taxes.** Do you want to file a joint tax return? If so, you need to remain married on December 31 of the year you wish to file jointly. If the matter is in the court after October 1 and if there is a signed settlement agreement, Judges can take whatever testimony of the spouses they need to conclude the matter and then hold off signing the final judgment until January 3. This enables parties to file joint returns in the year of the divorce.

- **Health Insurance.** Are you in need of coverage and the insurance company grace period is thirty days? Securing independent health insurance while you are still covered under a family plan means you don't have to risk having a medical matter which creates uninsured and uncovered medical expenses due to a gap in coverage.

Our society has not yet developed ceremonies to mark the end of a marriage. Often, a Judge can hear and finalize a divorce in as little as five minutes. A blink in the timeline of the marriage. This is the procedure. One spouse, the spouse who filed for divorce and is the Petitioner, appears

136

in court on the scheduled date at the scheduled time. The other spouse may or may not attend. Most divorce lawyers recommend that both spouses come to court on the day the divorce is going to be finalized but the Respondent does not have to appear.

On that date, the Judge will be on the bench. The Judge or his or her clerk will swear the Petitioner, the witness in the case. The Petitioner's lawyer will ask him or her a series of questions. The answers to the questions are evidence for the Judge. Those questions take about five minutes, sometimes longer, to be asked and answered. After those questions have been asked and the answers given, the Judge may ask some clarifying questions or he or she may just sign the final order dissolving the marriage. And after those five minutes in court, a very short period of time, the divorce is done and the marriage is over. It is very anticlimactic, so much so that many people feel shell-shocked that that is all it is.

Here's *a secret*. Prepare yourself mentally and emotionally for your day in court. Go to the courthouse any time that the Judge who has been assigned to your case is hearing other divorce cases. Sit in his or her courtroom. Courtrooms are a public place so you can be in the courtroom for as long as you like. Listen to what the lawyers say. Listen to what the Judge says. Watch and notice what the Judge likes or doesn't like. Get a perspective of what it will be like for you on the day you have to go to court for your divorce. Being there on a day you don't have to be makes being there on your day a lot easier because there will be no surprises.

Chapter Thirteen:
Dealing with Children during Divorce

The words spoken and the actions taken by parents are powerful examples for children. Those of divorcing parents leave lasting impressions and scars that children may carry into their adult lives. Children love their parents, both of their parents, even although one parent may think the other is "bad." They love their parents even when one is bad and perhaps was convicted of a crime. Children view their parents as the two people in the world who love them, take care of them and, most importantly, keep them safe from harm. It is during times of divorce that a parent's ability to love, to take care of and to keep their children safe from harm may be compromised or diminished.

Sometimes a parent will unintentionally hurt or neglect a child because that parent is in so much pain that they are unable to care for themselves, let alone care for the children. Sometimes parents will intentionally hurt or neglect a child in order to hurt their spouse. This behavior can have long-term negative effects on the child, including causing the child to have unsuccessful relationships in the future. Negative behavior includes the withholding of child support payments, the withholding of visitation between the parent and the child, the failure to return a child at the designated time, the hiding of personal assets or saying negative things about a spouse in casual conversations with friends within the earshot of the children.

Often a divorcing spouse often just wants to give up on the situation, the marriage, the spouse or their job. Divorces are as difficult or more trying on children. It seems obvious, but it isn't. Many adults believe that the children don't know about the divorce, are not affected by the divorce and will be fine after the divorce. This is BS. Adults with a lot more life experience have a difficult time with divorce. Children don't have the life experience, the intuition or the coping skills to be able to handle a divorce. Adults often exhibit behavioral problems or say or do hurtful things.

Divorce lawyers report that clients who are going through a divorce are "good people at their absolute worst." They scream and hit each other. There can be orders of protection or restraining orders and property is broken. Behavior occur that the same person would never do or imagine themselves doing if they were not in a divorcing situation. Imagine a child with ten years of life experience. They are even more likely to exhibit behavioral problems or say or do hurtful things. But if they throw a temper tantrum, we discipline them. If they break something, we make them replace it. It is no surprise then that the children are confused when the family has a double standard for behavior, one that applies to the adults and one that applies to the children.

The second way a parent can intentionally or unintentionally create problems for their child is when they do not know the difference between what age appropriate information is and what is not. Here is a common example. Mary Pat's husband Kevin had an affair with his assistant Scarlet.

Mary Pat was furious. She yelled at Kevin about it, she talked on the phone to her best friend Belle about it. She told Kevin that she was going to tell the children (ages 8 and 12) "the truth" about Kevin. Some people might be shocked about that, some people may agree with that. Most divorce lawyers will advise their client to get professional help.

The problem for the children is that until one of the spouses tells them that Mom or Dad has a girlfriend or boyfriend, the children don't know. To the spouse who has been violated because of the relationship, it is the monster who took their co-parent away. To the children, it is just another adult in their life. It is no different than if the children are introduced to a new coach, new teacher or new neighbor. At some point, they will be mad at Dad and may feel sorry for Mom. If they like Scarlet, they may get mad at Mom and feel sorry for Dad.

Another way it can happen is like this. Liam was furious that Kathleen wanted a divorce. He finally was resolved to it but did not want her to have any money. The court ordered Liam to pay half of the credit card bills and to pay child support to Kathleen. Every time Liam had the children he refused to take them anywhere. When they asked if he would take them to McDonald's, he refused, telling the children "I have no money. Your Mother took it all." Children don't understand the financial matters of the family. But at some point, they will begin to feel sorry for Dad and maybe even mad at Mom. They are likely to stop asking Dad for anything and may even begin to think they have to be his caretaker.

The behaviors the adults demonstrate do impact and make a difference in how well or how poorly a child survives a divorce. This is No BS.

Here are some useful do's and don'ts regarding children during a divorce:

1. **Do practice patience and encourage open, age-appropriate dialog.** Let the children express their feelings. Remind the children that both parents love them...no matter how much you want to be seen as the "good" parent. If your children ask questions about the divorce, answer in terms that are appropriate to your child's age and level of understanding. Don't give your children the "truth" as you would tell it to your best friend.

2. **Don't badmouth your spouse or partner, their parent.** Try to be civil and act with common courtesy to your former spouse in front of the children.

3. **Don't prevent children from seeing the other parent or the other parent's relatives.** Don't discipline the children with threats of "you can't go visit this weekend unless you...." Do try to stay geographically close to your ex-spouse.

4. **Do not expect or let the children be messengers of information between you and the other parent.**

Do not ask them to ask the other parent for something you are not willing to ask them for, no matter what the reason. Don't let the children report to you what your former spouse is doing, with whom.

HOUSE DIVIDED

Information coming into the home of married parents:

Information coming into the home of divorced parents:

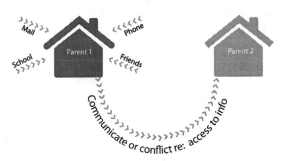

5. **Do keep the other parent advised and up-to-date on important matters relating to the children including school functions, extracurricular activities and special events.** Children like and need to be supported in their activities and social lives by both parents. Sports activities, time with friends, church and jobs, whether babysitting or

other forms of employment, are natural passages for many children. When both parents can provide support and encouragement to explore these avenues, even when the activities take time away from the parents, healthier, happier children will become better adjusted adults.

6. **If you are the parent without physical custody, do see or talk to your children at least once a week.** Maintain as many traditions, habits and rituals with your children as you can. Create new traditions. Do not attempt to buy your children's love or affection. Kids usually (OK, always) act in their own self interest. They may respond with enthusiasm, but ultimately these ploys may damage your relationship and their self-esteem.

7. **Do keep your children's pictures on the shelves in your home and keep their favorite toys or possessions around for them.** Give them the freedom to bring these things, their things, back and forth between their two homes.

8. **Do find professional help that you and your family are comfortable with.** Family counseling often helps manage the transitions, be it from home to home or from age group to age group. A third party can troubleshoot and find those difficult issues, the elephants in the room, that have been hard face and hard to talk about or resolve.

It's important to keep in mind that your children see and experience divorce differently than how you, as an adult, understand or experience divorce. No matter what their age, children have a limited ability to understand what is happening during a divorce, what they are feeling and why. That doesn't stop them, however, from trying to figure out "the big picture."

Younger children may see themselves as the cause of the divorce or a participant in events that led to the breakdown of the marriage. Younger children often blame themselves or invent imaginary reasons for their parents' separation and divorce. Some believe, "if only I had behaved better or helped Mom and Dad get along better, they would still be together." Some imagine that their parents will walk out the door and never come back again. Children may isolate themselves with the burden of these thoughts, becoming too afraid to tell anyone and, perhaps, believing they are the only ones in the world who feels this way.

Many children hope, wish or believe that their parents will get back together. Because of a child's limited ability to imagine or forecast the future, younger children cling to the only reality they know. It is not uncommon for even those children who have experienced or witnessed abuse to wish their parents would stay together. No matter what the circumstances, children develop a profound bond and a deep sense of loyalty to both parents.

Children learn and build their sense of self by watching and interacting with their parents. Children who witness parental arguing often experience it as although they are personally involved. Young children cannot separate themselves from their parents. Worse still, it is very hard for children to understand why the two most important people in their lives, on whom they depend for their very safety and survival, cannot get along. Children can't just leave the family when they argue with a sibling or friend, so why is it OK that Mom or Dad should move out and leave the family just because they have been arguing? When parents continually argue, their children get caught in the middle. They worry about having to take sides and about pleasing both parents—a very heavy burden for a young child.

Pre-teens and teenagers have a better ability to understand the problems that come up in a family but they too are without the life experience to have an accurate perspective of the situation. Developmentally, preteens and teenagers react differently through the changes that happen from a divorce. They tend to hold both their parents accountable for the divorce. They will most likely react to their parents' separation with anger. Older teenagers may wonder if they will be able to have a good relationship with someone. Some decide they will never marry. Teens often experience conflicting emotions and needs. They may be torn between wanting their independence but needing the protection of being in a family. They want their freedom from rules but need their parents' guidance on how to live. They want to be loved but want to be left alone.

Teenagers have some of the advantages of maturity and understanding of human relationships. However, this understanding makes them aware that life as they know it will change. They will anticipate housing, school and social life disruptions.

Most children worry about how the divorce will affect them, both now and in the future.

Like the adults who are getting divorced, anger is the most common emotion for children who are reacting to pain. Children, preteens and teenagers express it differently and are not given the luxury to express their anger and their fears in the same way as an adult would. Encourage them to talk about their feelings and to express disappointment and fears with a safe person, which may not be you. Let them give input in how to deal with changes that are likely to occur because of the divorce.

Having the appropriate conversation about separation and divorce at the proper time with both parents present is one of the hardest and most emotional steps in the process. Most parents cannot do it together and most cannot present the idea in the way that would be most beneficial for the children. How parents handle this crucial step can set the pattern for the trust and security children feel in the future. It is a challenge to communicate that neither of you will abandon the children, physically or emotionally, when you believe that that is exactly what your spouse is doing (or vice versa).

Just as telling your spouse or being told by your spouse that a separation or divorce was on the horizon set off a myriad of reactions for both of you, so too will telling your children that you are separating or getting a divorce. Those reactions can vary from confusion, fear, denial and sadness to anger, guilt and shock.

Take the time to prepare for this discussion. Handle this process thoughtfully and carefully. Decide where and when you will tell each child, whether it will be all together or separately. If appropriate and possible, the children do better when they hear the news from both parents at the same time. It is difficult to present a united front when telling the children. It is difficult to presenting the information without one parent beginning to blame the other for the divorce, even if it is as subtle as "Mommy doesn't want to be married any more" or "Daddy would rather work than be home." In those situations where the spousal relationship has deteriorated and is highly conflicted, the assistance of a therapist or minister is helpful.

Here are some suggestions:

- **Select a time and place to talk to your children.** Choose a time when you will be at your best, not a time when you are tired. Choose a place where your children will feel comfortable. It may or may not be in your home. If you are telling more than one child at the same time, have subsequent conversations with each child alone, especially if there is a significant age difference between them. Just like you trained them to tie their shoes or ride their bike, most children learn from several short talks, trial and error if you will, rather than digesting it all in one sitting.

- **Avoid ambushing the children.** Contrary to popular belief, immediately telling children or waiting to tell them will not protect children from anxiety. Most children know when something isn't right between their parents. They know if you fight a lot or don't talk a lot or that one of you is gone a lot.

- **Tell children, in general and age-appropriate terms, what they need to know, not what you think they should know.** Most children have no concept of what divorce means and they don't care. Children do what the parents require them to do. If the parents decide to move because they got a job change, they move. They don't ask the children if it's OK to move, to make a job change or to take a vacation. The children live with the change. They make new friends, they go to a new school. It just is. It is amazing that parents who are divorcing or separating think it is appropriate to make the children equal decision-makers. But they do.

When parents divorce, they involve the children in a lot of the decisions. They ask them who they want to live with; they ask them what they want to do. More often than not, it is the parents who are burdened and feel that they have to tell the children what divorce means. But really, why? The children don't get that voice in the courtroom, but parents often make children believe they get to choose or decide where they live. This occurs even when the parents are not able to decide and have left the ultimate decision up to the Judge. Now, I think that is real BS.

Children don't have a voice in the process and in my opinion, they shouldn't. And I know some readers will think that is BS. In my opinion the children don't have the life experience, the wisdom, the discernment, the motivation or the financial savvy to make a good decision for themselves or for their parents. Divorce lawyers see too many parents embark on extremely costly litigation just because their children wanted something. Adults compromise their ability to pay for children's college education or vacations or housing by paying lots of money to us lawyers. Think about what children really need and make the adult decision, despite what the children "say" they want. That is No BS.

There are many things children do need. They need to know that separation and divorce is not their fault. They need to know that separation and divorce is an adult problem that will be worked out by adults and that they will be informed when resolution is reached. They need to know that everything is fundamentally well and that when difficult times come, the adults will be able to handle them. Enough preaching...you get the idea!

Plan what to say ahead of time. Above all else, be genuine. Here are some messages that may be useful:

1. "We won't be living together anymore, but we both love you no matter where either of us lives."

2. "I/we know it seems unfair that these problems cause you pain and unhappiness. I/we wish things were different, too, but they're not and we all have to work at accepting the changes in our family."

3. "We will always be a family."

4. "Separation is Mom and Dad's issue. You are not to blame. It is our matter and we will work it out."

5. "I/we want you to say what you feel and think. You may feel worried, angry and hurt. I/we understand because your Mom/Dad and I often have these same feelings too."

Give your children opportunities to ask questions and share their thoughts and feelings. Some children may be afraid to ask questions or don't know how to express their ideas. Anticipate and ask questions that may be on their minds. Remember that children need time to digest this information too. Be prepared to revisit the discussion and let them know that you are willing to talk about things as often as they need or want to.

Some children will have suspected the divorce is imminent. For others, it will come as a complete shock. Some children may feel relieved that things are finally out in the open. Some will still feel vulnerable and insecure. Some will demonstrate no grief and others will express profound grief. And, it could be different on any given day. Still, most children, no matter what their age, will worry about what life will be like without both parents under the same roof. This is true no matter how strained or difficult family life may have been.

Do the things you love to do with your children and would have done if you stayed married. Here are some suggestions:

1. Give your children their spelling tests.

2. Do flash card drills for math.

3. Do a science experiment with your children.

4. Read your children a story, your favorite or theirs.

5. Do the dishes with your children. Tell them stories of your deprived childhood when you had to do this task without the aid of a dishwasher.

6. Help plan the school calendar and daily schedules.

7. Take your kids to a museum or historical site.

8. Hike with your children and talk about the woods, your childhood or their dreams.

9. Discuss current events at the dinner table (calmly, when possible).

10. Read their essays and offer praise and constructive suggestions.

11. Watch the children when your former spouse needs your assistance.

12. Play silly games that involve lots of hugging and wrestling.

13. Take your children to your childhood neighborhood and give them a tour of your memories.

14. Express genuine delight when they draw a picture for you. Put the pictures in a place that shows the children you are proud of them.

15. Plant a garden together.

16. Teach them to strive for excellence in their chores, their studies and their work.

17. Watch your boys play baseball and your daughters perform ballet with equal enthusiasm.

18. Ask them what they want to be when they grow up.

19. Tell them what you wanted to be when you grew up.

20. Love them to the very best of your ability.

Chapter Fourteen:
You Might Need to Do Drugs....
Your Mental, Physical and
Spiritual Health

The decision to divorce or separate is not one that happens overnight; in fact, it can take years. Divorce and filing for divorce takes its toll on almost every aspect of your life —physical, financial, mental, emotional and spiritual.

EMOTIONAL TIMELINE

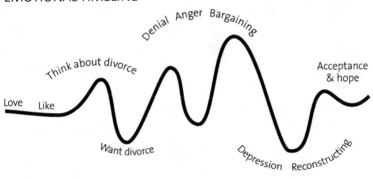

Divorce is a difficult, stressful and painful process. We know stress comes from imminent life changes, uncertainty and unresolved issues. Naturally divorce and separation, which create all of those, are not easy. Stressors can include illogical people, insensitive people and sudden changes.

Most people actually grieve during a divorce. Divorce causes the loss of many things: the dream, the marriage, the relationship, the relationships tied to the relationship, the prestige. In many ways, it is a death.

Be quick to see where the mental health professionals can properly diagnose your ability to cope with and handle the temporary (and normal) depression that occurs in most people going through a divorce. For some people, short-term medication in the form of an anti-depressant may make dealing with the very difficult issues and changes easier.

Psychologists have identified the phases of grief and similarly the phases of divorce as denial, anger, bargaining, depression and acceptance. One must go through each phase to be able to move on successfully with life. Some say stress is resistance to reality. A University of Iowa study provides some useful definitions of the effects of stages of grief which can easily be applied to the effects of a divorce.

Denial, numbness and shock. These emotions serve to protect the individual from experiencing the intensity of the loss. Individuals may ruminate about what could have been done to prevent the loss. Individuals can become preoccupied about ways things could have been better, imagining all the things that will never be. Depression, feelings of loneliness, emptiness, isolation and self-pity can also surface during this phase.

Anger. This reaction usually occurs when an individual feels helpless and powerless. Anger may result from feeling abandoned.

Guilt. Whether you wanted it or not, at some point it

is natural to feel guilty about the divorce. You may feel "I should have done more." Feelings of guilt are usually not in your best interest or those of your children. Guilt may add to an already deep sense of personal loss and sadness and may provoke self-destructive thoughts or destructive thoughts of others.

Acceptance. The passage of time allows the individual an opportunity to resolve the range of feelings that surface and ultimately move on.

The Divorce Diet. Because the physical toll on a person is so great during a divorce, references are frequently made to "the divorce diet." The phenomenon of losing a significant amount of weight as a reaction to the trauma of a divorce is common. During this time, people who take good care of themselves, get regular exercise, make healthy food choices and take proper medication fare better than those who don't.

Spirituality. For some, coping with the immense effects of a divorce can only come from a Higher Power. *The Serenity Prayer* and the *Prayer of St. Francis* are prayers spouses in the divorce process often rely on.

The Serenity Prayer

"God grant me the serenity to accept the things I cannot change, the courage to change the things I can and the wisdom to know the difference."

Reinhold Niebuhr

Accept what is, as it is. Not as easy as it sounds.

The Prayer of St. Francis

"Make me an instrument of peace.

Where there is hatred, let me sow love;
Where there is injury, pardon;
Where there is doubt, faith;
Where there is despair, hope;
Where there is darkness, light;
and where there is sadness, joy.

Grant that I may not so much seek
To be consoled as to console;
To be understood as to understand;
To be loved as to love.
For it is in giving that we receive;
It is in pardoning that we are pardoned."

Turn the other cheek, really not as easy as it sounds.

For those who are spiritually minded, having a mantra like *The Serenity Prayer* or the *Prayer of St. Francis* creates calm and provides the opportunity to slow down. Mantra's such as these also help maintain emotional balance in the midst of turmoil.

For those looking for a less spiritual approach, here are some tips from other experts.

1. Take full responsibility for your life and your actions.

2. Figure out what's not working in your life and stop doing it. Figure out what works better and start doing that instead.

3. Learn what you can from your divorce and apply it to your evolution as a human being.

4. Believe that the life you want post-divorce is a possible reality.

5. Create a vision of life after divorce and focus on it.

6. Take action, a little every day, to get you to where you want to go.

7. Make conscious and positive life choices.

8. Take extremely good care of yourself and your children.

9. Expect to be human. Nothing more or less.

Chapter Fifteen:
The Family Forward

After the Divorce is Done, Post Decree Checklist/ Tips

The divorce is done, the papers are signed and the Judge has signed everything. It's finished, right? WRONG. Thinking everything is finished just because the papers are signed is BS. There are a lot of loose ends to tie up to really get everything finished and to start to get your life in order. Here are some of the things to check and to do to really be done:

1. **Verify that all joint credit card accounts are closed.** Change all credit card accounts that you or your spouse will retain to your individual accounts.

2. **Verify that all joint bank accounts are closed.** Reopen accounts as individual accounts.

3. **Change all utility accounts to the proper spouse's name.** Verify that your name has been removed from utility accounts for which you are no longer responsible.

4. **If you are moving, send out a notice** of your new address and phone number to all family, friends, creditors, banking institutions, etc.

5. **Change your legal documents and papers from your married name to your maiden name, if desired.** If you changed your name, keep a certified copy of your Divorce Decree or name change order so you can provide a copy to:
   - Bank(s)
   - Social Security Office
   - Secretary of State-Drivers License Division

6. **Notify your creditors.** Pay the bills you agreed to pay on time.

7. **Obtain the original Property Deed and Quit Claim Deed** for the residential property and record it with the Recorder of Deeds.

8. **Obtain title(s) to vehicles retained by you.** Apply for new title(s) at the Secretary of State's Office or a local currency exchange.

9. **Move any personal property out of a joint safety deposit box to a new safety deposit box.**

10. **Prepare the necessary paperwork (which may involve on-going legal proceedings) for transfer of retirement benefits to the recipient (i.e. pension accounts).**

11. **Obtain automobile insurance for your vehicle.** Verify that you are not carrying or paying for insurance for vehicles retained by your former spouse.

12. **Check your credit report for adverse listings.** If there are any adverse listings, write a 100-word, one-page explanation to the Credit Bureau notifying them of your divorce.

13. **Shop around for the best prices for medical benefits and obtain medical insurance.**

14. **Change the life insurance beneficiaries** or at least remove your former spouse (unless you are required to keep that spouse listed for child support purposes).

15. **Change your Last Will and Testament.** Be sure your will, power of attorney for health care and general power of attorney are in order and that you have designated the person you wish to handle your affairs in your absence.

Chapter Sixteen:
General Wisdom

Divorce is difficult. It can be complicated by friends, family and a variety of other issues. Here are some of my best tips, the secrets if you will, to get divorced successfully. By successfully, I mean never having to litigate with this partner again.

- **Use an experienced family law attorney,** one that practices in the county or region where you will be getting a divorce. He or she will be able to give you the representation you need and will be able to look out for your best interests.

- **Listen to your attorney.**

- **Don't let your friends or family members tell you what to do....even if they are paying for it.** Although they mean well, they are not experienced in the laws that govern divorces. Listen to your attorney. He or she knows more than your friends.

- **Confide in three good friends,** the ones you trust enough to tell you the truth and to whom you will actually listen.

- **Document what you need.** Documenting everything is obsessive. Document the things that you and your attorney think will be important later on. Keep a journal of important dates and events. Use the No BS Divorce Workbook to keep track of your questions and the answers you get to them.

- **Do not have an affair** while you are in the process of getting a divorce.

- **Date after you're divorced,** but don't flaunt it.

- **Don't go on Match.com or any similar sites.**

- **Don't get pregnant…**(it's happened).

- **Learn from this divorce and the past.** Use the techniques and skills you have which have worked in the past when you wanted to make your spouse do something they didn't want to do.

- **Fix what you can and then let go of what you can't.**

Prologue

Mother Teresa Did Know Best

After witnessing and participating in thousands of divorce cases, I have come to believe that people create their own difficulty in a divorce. They delegate their power to lawyers, family, friends and their children. They don't do what they need to do when they need to do it. They do what they shouldn't do when they shouldn't do it. They are afraid to face reality or naively think that the divorce will never happen. They fail to get the right expert help they need.

It is hard for someone to get out from underneath the incredible pressure of a divorce. It is hard to take the proper actions with limited skill, talent and vision. Those people who rely on their outside resources and internal spiritual intuition for guidance often do better getting through a divorce. Having a spiritual core and paying attention to your intuition yields far better results not only in the courtroom but also in life generally.

When it's all over, the divorce is done, the dust has settled and the lawyers, therapists and all other professionals have come and gone. The family then lives with the consequences of the decisions made. Being an active participant, making the decisions you can make and relying on the expert's advice for those decisions which are beyond your ability, yields better decisions and agreements. It is your future, your life, not ours.

167

In closing, I would like to leave you with the words and wisdom of Mother Teresa:

"People are often unreasonable,
illogical and self-centered.
Forgive them anyway.
If you are kind, people may accuse you of
selfish ulterior motives.
Be kind anyway.
If you are successful, you will win some false friends
and some true enemies.
Succeed anyway.
If you are honest and frank, people may cheat you.
Be honest and frank anyway.
What you spend years building, someone could destroy overnight.
Build anyway.
If you find serenity and happiness, they may be jealous.
Be happy anyway.
The good you do today, people will often forget tomorrow.
Do good anyway.
Give the world the best you have and it may never be enough.
Give the world the best you have anyway."

"You see, in the final analysis it is between you and God.
It was never between you and them anyway."

Mother Teresa

I send you my very best wishes for a successful resolution
of your difficulties and a life after divorce
beyond your wildest dreams.

Brigid

Do you have a BS Belief that we should include in the Second Edition?

If so, e-mail it to Brigid@BrigidDuffield.com and we'll clarify it for you...and maybe add to it our next edition of the *No BS Divorce!*

Professional and Community Seminars

Brigid A. Duffield is available to speak to professional and community groups. Presentations can be customized. Programs include:

- Divorce and the Holidays...When its Not Such a Wonderful Life
- 'Til Death Do Us Part and Other Marriage Myths
- Alcohol & Family Law Practice, a Kaleidoscope of Multifaceted Issues
- At Risk: Colleagues in Crisis, Recognizing Alcohol Impairment in the Professional
- Conflict Resolution in the Divorce Process
- Mediation as an Alternate to the Adversary Process

Contact Legally Speaking, Inc. at 630.221.9300.

Save on Quantity Orders

Attorneys, therapists, financial planners and other professionals are invited to provide *No BS Divorce, Secrets of a Divorce Attorney,* to clients to help them through the difficult period surrounding divorce.

Quantity ordered	Discount
10 -24	10%
25 - 99	15%
100 or more	20%

Also available, *No BS Divorce Workbook*

As a companion to the *No BS Divorce, Secrets of a Divorce Attorney,* the *No BS Divorce Workbook* is a valuable tool to anyone contemplating or going through the divorce process. Use the workbook to record questions for your attorney, inventory your assets, calculate your net worth and keep notes.

Order at www.brigidduffield.com or call 630.221.9300.